2007

THE BEST 10-MINUTE PLAYS
FOR THREE OR MORE ACTORS

Smith and Kraus's
Short Plays and 10-Minute Play Collections

Christopher Durang Vol. I: 27 Short Plays

Frank D. Gilroy Vol. II: 15 One-Act Plays

Israel Horovitz Vol. I: 16 Short Plays

Romulus Linney 17 Short Plays

Terrence McNally Vol. I: 15 Short Plays

Lanford Wilson: 21 Short Plays

Act One Festival 1995: The Complete One-Act Plays

Act One Festival 1994: The Complete One-Act Plays

EST Marathon 1999: The Complete One-Act Plays

EST Marathon 1998: The Complete One-Act Plays

EST Marathon 1997: The Complete One-Act Plays

EST Marathon 1996: The Complete One-Act Plays

EST Marathon 1995: The Complete One-Act Plays

EST Marathon 1994: The Complete One-Act Plays

HB Playwrights Short Play Festival, 1997–2003 Festival Editions

Twenty One-Acts from 20 Years at the Humana Festival 1975–1995

The Women's Project and Productions Rowing to America and Sixteen Other
    Short Plays

8 TENS @ 8 Festival: 30 10-Minute Plays from the Santa Cruz Festivals I–VI

30 Ten-Minute Plays from the Actors Theatre of Louisville for 2 Actors

30 Ten-Minute Plays from the Actors Theatre of Louisville for 3 Actors

30 Ten-Minute Plays from the Actors Theatre of Louisville for 4, 5, and 6 Actors

2004: The Best 10-Minute Plays for Two Actors

2004: The Best 10-Minute Plays for Three or More Actors

2005: The Best 10-Minute Plays for Two Actors

2005: The Best 10-Minute Plays for Three or More Actors

2006: The Best 10-Minute Plays for Two Actors

2006: The Best 10-Minute Plays for Three or More Actors

2007

THE BEST 10-MINUTE PLAYS
FOR THREE OR MORE ACTORS

Edited by Lawrence Harbison
Foreword by D. L. Lepidus

CONTEMPORARY PLAYWRIGHT SERIES

A Smith and Kraus Book
Hanover, New Hampshire

Published by Smith and Kraus, Inc.
177 Lyme Road, Hanover, NH 03755
www.SmithandKraus.com
(888) 282-2881

First Edition: April 2008
10 9 8 7 6 5 4 3 2 1

Manufactured in the United States of America
Cover and text design by Julia Hill Gignoux, Freedom Hill Design
Cover photo by Trevor Stefanick: (left to right) Nancy Quasarano, Preston Misner, and Will Elwood in *If, When, and Only* by Maryann Lesert.

ISBN 978-1-57525-590-3
ISSN 1550-6754
Library of Congress Control Number: 2008923277

Contents

Foreword

The ten-minute play as an accepted dramatic form is a fairly recent development. Some would say that its popularity is a result of our diminished attention spans, which may be partially true; but here's how the genre came to be.

For several years, Actors Theatre of Louisville, under the leadership of Jon Jory, commissioned playwrights to write plays of short duration for performance by its apprentice company. This was a way for the theater to do something to help playwrights, but also it was a way to develop relationships with them, many of which bore fruit over the years as these writers went on to have full-length plays staged in Actors Theater's famed Humana Festival.

Over the years, Actors Theatre built up quite a library of these short plays, all of them in manuscript. An editor for the play publisher Samuel French got the idea that maybe other theaters, actors, and students might be interested in these plays if they were made available to them. He managed to swing a deal for French to publish an anthology of Actors Theatre's best short plays, which they were now calling "ten-minute plays." This anthology was so successful that French has now published six such volumes, and most of the other publishers have followed suit, including Smith and Kraus, as its annual ten-minute play anthologies will attest. Bills of ten-minute plays are now produced regularly — and all over the world.

There are some who feel that the ten-minute play ought to be an opportunity for playwrights to experiment — with language, with form, with character, with subject matter. "The best" ten-minute plays are therefore the ones that depart the most from conventional drama. For the purposes of this series, here is how I define best: that which is most useful to people who will buy this book and produce these plays. Some actors and directors prefer straightforward realism; whereas others go for more abstract, experimental plays. I don't carry a torch for any one style, so I have tried to include in this book examples of realism and, shall we say, "nonrealism." I hope you will find herein more than one play that rings your bell. They all rang mine.

Most of the plays in this book are by exciting up-and-comers, such as Melanie Marnich, Diana Amsterdam, Jenny Lyn Bader, Estep Nagy, Nora Chau, and Kevin Six.

Should you find a play (or plays) in this book that you want to produce, you will find information in the back on who to contact for performance rights.

After seven years of doing these books for Smith and Kraus, I have decided to step aside and have turned over the reins to my old pal Lawrence Harbison, who knows as much about the theater and its plays and playwrights as anyone I know. It has been a very rewarding and very challenging task editing these anthologies; but now it is time to hang up my red pencil. I am retiring to Myrtle Beach, there to become one of those geezers who stands around all day in a kilt, sending foursomes of awful golfers off the first tee. In my free time I won't be reading plays: I'll be taking up bungee jumping, hang gliding, and alligator wrestling. There is life beyond the theater.

D. L. Lepidus
Myrtle Beach, South Carolina

PLAYS FOR
THREE ACTORS

Bluebeard

GEORGE FREEK

The play was produced by the American Stage Theatre
Company (211 3rd Street S, St. Petersburg, Fla.) at the
Large Cultural Center January 25–February 4 in their
10x10 New Play Festival.

CHARACTERS
FREDERICK: a literature professor, thirties
DENISE: his wife, a literature professor, thirties
ANGIE: a waitress, twenties

SETTING
A restaurant cocktail lounge; midwestern college city of 160,000

TIME
Recently

. . .

The lounge area of an elegant restaurant. Frederick and Denise sit at a table.

DENISE: I'm really perplexed. I mean I'm pleased, naturally. We don't normally have lunch at a place like this, and champagne, too! I feel appropriately decadent. But what is it all for?
FREDERICK: *(Proposing a toast.)* Well, for one thing, happy anniversary.
DENISE: Oh my. But that's really not for another couple days.
FREDERICK: I know that. But if I'd waited until then, it wouldn't have been a surprise.
DENISE: Well, it's wonderful! Thank you!
FREDERICK: I suppose I should make some kind of toast. "Mud in your eye" doesn't quite do it. Suppose I simply tell you how much I love you and how much I have appreciated four wonderful years?
DENISE: I think that would be perfect, darling. Well, to us! *(They drink.)*
FREDERICK: Did I ever tell you my mother wanted me to become a priest?
DENISE: That would have been inconvenient.
FREDERICK: There was also a major problem. I mean I'm an atheist.
DENISE: And you wouldn't have been able to marry me, either.
FREDERICK: Well, Mom and Dad never got along very well. In fact, I remember one time she took after him with a butcher knife, and he was defending himself with my tricycle, so she didn't see not being married as a serious problem.
DENISE: Oh come on, I know your mother. She's a very sweet lady.
FREDERICK: She is NOW, but people aren't always what they seem. I'm afraid, sweetheart, sometimes you are very naïve.
DENISE: Mm . . . and is that such a terrible thing?

FREDERICK: No. In fact, sometimes it can be very charming.

DENISE: Thank you.

FREDERICK: But there are other times when it can be dangerous.

DENISE: My! That sounds like a confession. What! Are you telling me I married a Bluebeard?

FREDERICK: Nooo!

DENISE: Good.

FREDERICK: I hope I'm not as bad as that.

DENISE: Well, I don't think you are, at least not today.

FREDERICK: No, sweetheart, I'm not Bluebeard, but I am human.

DENISE: Well, I really hope so.

FREDERICK: But anniversary aside, there's also another reason I wanted you to meet me for lunch.

DENISE: Oh? Now that also sounds a little portentous, darling.

FREDERICK: Well, I do have something to tell you, Denise. I didn't have to tell you, and you probably never would have found out. But I felt like I should tell you. It just seemed like the right thing to do.

DENISE: After that, I'm not sure if I want you to tell me.

FREDERICK: Look, do you remember when I went to that conference in Chicago, and I decided to stay in the city Saturday night?

DENISE: Well of course I do. It was only a month or two ago. You wanted to attend that seminar on Oscar Wilde because you're teaching him in the fall. But . . . Good Lord, Frederick, you're not going to tell me you suddenly discovered you're gay, are you!

FREDERICK: It might be easier to tell you if that was it.

DENISE: *(She stares at him.)* I think you'd better just tell me.

FREDERICK: Denise, sweetheart, first, I want you to know how much I love you.

DENISE: I hope I already know that. You mentioned it in your anniversary toast.

FREDERICK: I said I decided to tell you this because it's the right thing to do, but now that I'm trying to say it, I find it's much harder than I thought. And I also want you to know that however much you might hate me after I tell you, you can't hate me as much as I hate myself! God . . . I sincerely hope you can believe that, Denise . . . *(He chokes back a sob.)* . . .

DENISE: For heaven's sake! Frederick, what is this? Are you going to tell me you slept with another woman in Chicago?

FREDERICK: You mean you already knew! But how did you find out! Did

Norman tell you? Christ, that bastard! I told him I wanted to tell you myself —

DENISE: What are you saying? You mean that you . . . You did? You had sex with . . . some woman!

FREDERICK: Look, it's not what you're thinking!

DENISE: It's not what I'm thinking? All right . . . What AM I thinking!

FREDERICK: You're angry. Of course you are! And you have every right to be! I understand that!

DENISE: I'm angry? Well, yes, I suppose I am! I don't know! I don't know what I'm feeling. I'm . . . shocked! And I'm . . . I'm hurt!

FREDERICK: *(A sudden angry outburst.)* All right, I understand that! But I didn't have to tell you about it! There is probably no way you would have ever found out, but the point is I felt like I had to do the right thing —

DENISE: So then, I suppose I should find that . . . admirable.

FREDERICK: Admirable! OK, I know I deserve that sarcasm, and I'm sure at this moment, whatever else you are feeling, you probably hate my guts. But I want you to know that no matter how disgusted you are with me, you couldn't possibly be as disgusted with me as I am with myself! *(He appears to choke back more sobs.)*

DENISE: *(At a loss.)* But dar . . . Frederick, how did it happen? Who was she? I mean if I knew what happened, then maybe I could . . . understand? I mean was this with . . . Was she a —

FREDERICK: A prostitute! God! You must despise me! Well, I don't blame you! Slap me, Denise!

DENISE: What!

FREDERICK: I mean it! Slap me! Please! Kick me in the balls! In front of everyone! That's exactly what I deserve! And I only hope you never experience the amount of self-loathing I'm now experiencing! *(He again appears to choke back sobs.)* Well, if you want to know how it happened, I'll try to explain. After the seminars on Saturday, a group of us went for dinner and then we went into the lounge for a few drinks. Well, we all had way too many drinks. Frankly, I got drunk. Believe me, I'm not offering it as an excuse! There is no excuse! Anyway, Angie was the waitress in the restaurant, and after dinner she was sitting in the lounge, too. Norman and the rest of the group had left, and I was finishing up my last drink when I discovered she was sitting next to me. I won't deny I was flattered. But the thing is she was very upset. It seems her mother had just died a few days earlier, and they'd been very close. Well, probably because I was drunk, I felt I had to give her some comfort. And she was so upset . . . She said she didn't want to be alone, and so I took her to her room. Frankly, I was afraid she might do something foolish . . . And so then . . . Well, I did something foolish! Oh the hell with it, Denise, why don't you just file for a divorce!

DENISE: Divorce! We've only been married four years!

FREDERICK: I know, but I promise you, if that's what you want, I won't cause trouble!

DENISE: *(She looks distraught.)* Oh God! Right now I just don't want to talk about this any longer!

FREDERICK: I understand. And I . . . I'm too ashamed to even say I'm sorry! *(He looks away, tearfully.)*

DENISE: *(Pause.)* Listen, Frederick, I'm going to go home now.

FREDERICK: All right. I don't blame you. You need to get away from me!

DENISE: It's not that. I'm going to OUR home, Frederick, and, well . . . I'll expect you for dinner.

FREDERICK: Denise, are you trying to tell me you . . . ? Are you saying that you might be able to . . . ?

DENISE: I . . . I don't know, Frederick. I . . . I do love you. *(She exits on the verge of tears.)*

(After Denise exits, Angie comes over to the table and embraces Frederick.)

ANGIE: I guess you told her?

FREDERICK: God, that was unpleasant. *(They sit down.)*

ANGIE: What did she say?

FREDERICK: I'm afraid if I tell you, it will only upset you.

ANGIE: You're telling me she was, like, that MEAN?

FREDERICK: I've already told you that the woman is an incredible bitch!

ANGIE: But didn't you tell her we're in love?

FREDERICK: Do you think that would matter to her?

ANGIE: God! Like how selfish can she be! She's really put you through hell, hasn't she, Freddy! *(She takes his hand.)* But she isn't going to cause trouble over your divorce, is she?

FREDERICK: Trouble! She intends to take me for everything I have!

ANGIE: Oh maan! But can she do that?

FREDERICK: She has promised me she will try.

ANGIE: Oh, Freddy, I'm so sorry! I feel like I've really screwed up your life!

FREDERICK: Don't say that, Angie! You're the best thing that's ever happened to me!

ANGIE: But NOW what's going to happen?

FREDERICK: Well, among other things, I assume she will drag us both through the mud. Naturally, she'll get the house and everything else! And I'm sure that I'll be fired from my job —

ANGIE: But . . . that is like totally shitty!

FREDERICK: The trouble is SHE will seem like the injured party.

ANGIE: God! If people could only see her for what she really is!

FREDERICK: Be prepared for living hell, sweetheart! She will make our life miserable. She will try to destroy us both, but I suppose there's no backing down at this point!

ANGIE: Are you sure?

FREDERICK: What are you suggesting?

ANGIE: I mean I can't stand to see you suffer like this, Freddy!

FREDERICK: But . . . I mean we can't just go on as we have been, um . . . can we?

ANGIE: I don't know what to say, Freddy. What do you think?

FREDERICK: Well, I know our life together will be a living hell, but I don't care how much garbage she throws at us, sweetheart, I love you and I'm simply going to barge straight ahead, no matter what she does!

ANGIE: Do you really mean that?

FREDERICK: Well . . . Yes . . . I mean if that's what you really want.

ANGIE: Oh, Freddy, I'm so glad to hear you say that!

FREDERICK: You are!

ANGIE: Yes, because there's something I've got to tell you —

FREDERICK: *(Interrupting, barely hearing her.)* Of course you do realize how miserable Denise will make things for us! She will be relentless —

ANGIE: *(Interrupting, not hearing him.)* I'm going to have a baby!

FREDERICK: *(He looks at her.)* You're . . . You are . . .

ANGIE: I was afraid to tell you. You might not want it, but now I know everything's OK!

FREDERICK: Then . . . you . . . You're . . . serious?

ANGIE: Yeah, babe! Isn't it like wonderful! *(She takes his hand.)*

FREDERICK: You're . . . absolutely sure?

ANGIE: I'm so happy! After what you said, I know everything will be fine. As long as we're together, everything will be wonderful!

(She smiles. He stares at her. Blackout.)

END OF PLAY

A Boy A Bat A Ball

MELANIE MARNICH

A Boy A Bat A Ball was originally presented by Mile Square Theatre in their 3rd Annual 7th Inning Stretch: 7 10-minute plays about baseball. Chris O'Connor, artistic director, June 18, 2005, at the DeBaun Auditorium, Hoboken, N.J. The director was Lenard Petit. The cast was as follows: Grandpa — Stanley Harrison; Dad — Christopher Petit; Son — Raymond McAnally; Announcer — Bryant Mason.

CHARACTERS

GRANDPA: mid-seventies

DAD: early forties

SON: nine-ish. Should be played by an adult actor, maybe early twenties. A five o'clock shadow is just fine for our purposes.

ANNOUNCER: any age in announcer years is OK. Present in voice only. Needs to be virtuosic.

SETTING

In the stands of an outdoor baseball stadium, probably not the good seats.

The strongest thing baseball has going for it today are its yesterdays.

—Ritter

Baseball was made for kids, and grown-ups only screw it up.

—Bob Lemon

•   •   •

Lights up. Grandpa, Dad, and Son are standing as the end of the National Anthem rings out. " . . . the la-and of the free-eeeeeee and the hooooome of the braaaaaaaaave." The stadium erupts in applause then quiets to the din of a ballpark. The guys sit. Grandpa and Dad have hot dogs and beer. Son has cotton candy and a huge supersized-oversized soda.

SON: Hey, Gramps, get this.

(He chugs some soda and burps the alphabet — or as much of it as possible.) BbbrruuABCDEFGHIJKLMNOPQRSTUVWXYZeeeeurp.

DAD: *(To Grandpa.)* In case you were wondering what twenty thousand bucks a year and a fancy Catholic school will get you these days.

SON: I can fart Ave Maria.

GRANDPA: That I'd like to hear.

(Son puffs up to toot the song.)

DAD: Don't even —

(Son waits, fully puffed.)

DAD: — think about it.

(Son deflates and focuses on his cotton candy and soda.)

GRANDPA: Wow, it's been years since I been to a game. *Years.*

DAD: Yeah, when you mentioned that I thought to myself "Hey, maybe I oughta take Dad to a game . . . " We used to go, you and me, back in the day. Kind of a tradition.

GRANDPA: It's a beautiful thing, tradition.

DAD: Exactly. And it's perfect for some father-son . . . Some father-son . . . Some . . . thing. Some togetherness. Or something. Right?

GRANDPA: Tradition and nostalgia. Get to be my age, and you love 'em both. Look at it. The diamond, the dugouts, the crowd. It takes a man back, you know? What a great game. What a . . .

(As he puts on his glasses.)

What the hell's all that?

DAD: All what?

GRANDPA: All that crap. Back there. Past center field. And right field. And left field.

DAD: That? Back there?

GRANDPA: Yeah. It looks like a . . . mall. A mall in the outfield.

DAD: Oh, no no no, Pops. That's not a mall. Just signage and endorsements made to *look* like a mall.

GRANDPA: In the park?

DAD: Yeah. Subtlety is a thing of the past, Pops. They tried it, and it didn't work. Now it's just balls-to-the-walls merchandising and marketing. Makes you wonder what we looked at before all this became available, doesn't it?

GRANDPA: We looked at the *game.*

DAD: Yeah, well, welcome to the game in the twenty-first century.

GRANDPA: Where have I been? Dead? I don't remember any of this.

DAD: I'll tell ya, the world of sports can change while you're having a Senior Moment. It's moving that fast.

GRANDPA: But this feels sort of . . .

DAD: Extreme?

GRANDPA: Well, yeah. I mean, I've watched baseball on TV sort of recently and I don't remember any of *this.*

DAD: This park is one-of-a-kind. See, the city passed a bill. We voted to become a test market for this sort of thing. It's about competition. About letting corporations be as aggressive as they want to be as a way of leveling the playing field. The biggest, the strongest, the most powerful wins. It's how the game is played. It's a beautiful thing.

GRANDPA: It's excessive and tasteless.

DAD: But, man, does it work. Chuck out all regulation and see how far, how fast a business can grow. It applies to the players, too.

GRANDPA: Like, with endorsements?

DAD: No. Like with "roids." And I don't mean hemorrhoids.

GRANDPA: *(With growing incredulity and confusion.)* But that's illegal. Last time I checked, completely illegal.

DAD: Not in this town, Pops. See, part of the bill we passed allows the players to operate like those companies. Let these guys steroid themselves to the gills and see how good they get. See them reach their full human potential with no one telling them "no." It's the all new all-American way.

GRANDPA: That's *insane.*

DAD: That's progress, Pops.

ANNOUNCER: It's a beautiful day for a ball game here at Wal-Mart-Home-Depot-Miller-Light-Levitra-Viagra-Prozac-Maybelline Park, everyone. A beautiful day for a game . . .

(Grandpa blinks in confusion . . .)

(Lights shift. Quickly. Time passes. Quickly.)

ANNOUNCER: . . . And now, at the bottom of the 9*th*, that makes the score a competitive 37 to 38. A real white-knuckle ride here at Wal-Mart-Home-Depot-Miller-Light-Levitra-Viagra-Prozac-Maybelline Park, folks.

GRANDPA: *(Still confused, but attempting normalcy.)* So. Hey. Stevie. What grade are you in now? Eleventh? Twelfth?

SON: Third.

GRANDPA: *(Shocked, of course.)* What?!

SON: Turned nine three weeks ago. You forgot.

GRANDPA: But you're so . . . *mature* for your age.

DAD: It's the vitamins. Great vitamins. He plays Little League, and they want him to be in tip-top shape. In case he wants to play in middle school. Kids have to be competitive, you know.

SON: Randy Stein's dad says they're not vitamins they're bovine growth hormones in chewable form.

DAD: *(As an insult.)* Randy Stein's dad listens to public radio.

GRANDPA: I haven't been nine for a long time, but as far as I can remember, we didn't have to *shave.*

DAD: *(As an explanation.)* Kids today.

GRANDPA: Honestly, have I been in a coma?

DAD: No. In a retirement community in Florida. Same thing if you don't watch it, Pops. And while you were pruning your orchids or learning tai chi or whatever it is you do down there, the world changed big-time.

ANNOUNCER: And the bases are loaded, folks. You can cut the tension with a spork here at Wal-Mart-Home-Depot-et-cetera-et-cetera-et-cetera Park.

SON: Hey Dad hey Dad hey hey. The other guy's up the other guy's up the other guy's up. He's up he's up.

ANNOUNCER: *Orlando's at the plate. Here comes the pitch aaaannnndddd-*
(The crack of the bat.)
(As the Announcer describes the action below, Grandpa, Dad, and Son follow the ball in play. Synchronized, choreographed heads and eyeballs.)

ANNOUNCER: A line drive! Larson grabs it on one hop and rifles it down the line to Jacobs at first! Tag!, Orlando is out! Jacobs fires it to Magill at third, Duke is OUT!, Magill powers it to Kennedy at second who is . . . now . . . blasting it home to Tellerico who catches it in midair! It's a quadruple play fans! Yes, four-count-em-four outs and they only needed ONE! Why did they do it? Because they could! And that, ladies and gentlemen, boys and girls, is the beauty and the purpose and God-given power of performance-enhancing drugs! Wait — What — What's this? Tellerico just pelted the ball out to the audience . . . looks like a fan is going to catch it . . . he does . . . and the ball . . . TAKES HIS ARM OFF!!! Can you believe it! Amazing! The power behind that ball. Tellerico is a champ! Whatta day, whatta play! Four outs and an involuntary amputation. Beats the hell outta bobble-head day, folks!

GRANDPA: The most beautiful sport in the world has officially become science fiction.

(And he takes a supersized drink from his supersized beer.)

DAD: You shoulda seen the sextuple they pulled last week against Baltimore. Seems like the sky's the limit and you gotta love it. I mean, the crack of the bat is the new sound of the future. Amazing, isn't it? Pops? Isn't it?

SON: Grandpa? You OK?

GRANDPA: No. I'm not OK. I'm not even close to OK.

DAD: Heart attack? Heat stroke? These things tend to happen here.

GRANDPA: No. I've completely overdosed on this bullshit and I've had it up to here. And *no* the crack of the bat is *not* the sound of the future.

DAD: It's not?

SON: It's not?

(The world sort of changes as Grandpa takes control of it, casting a bit of a spell, rousing and inspiring.)

GRANDPA: No, it's not, men. Get a grip on yourselves. It's the sound of a collective memory. Of our true anthem. Of kids in the sun. Of kids in the

lot, in the street, in the grass, in the park. Of the game. Like it should
be played. Like we three played it.

*(Dad takes the beer out of Grandpa's hands like "ooooh, guess who drank too
much." But Grandpa is utterly sober.)*

GRANDPA: Can you hear it?

(The crack of a bat.)

DAD: Like when I played?

(The crack of a bat.)

SON: Like when I played?

(The crack of a bat.)

GRANDPA: Yes.

SON: *(The spell coming over him.)* Like the other day I was running for the ball
across the grass across the outfield and there was like a movie in my
mind of players from a way long time ago cool like that.

DAD: *(The spell coming over him.)* Like when I played ball across from the
school with boys before they became men who forgot that they were ever
boys.

GRANDPA: Like when it was me and my friends and we'd play in the rain.
We'd play in the snow. We'd play and play and play.

DAD: And I smell the fear of the catcher.

SON: The fear of the dirt around the plate.

GRANDPA: But I'm not afraid.

DAD: I'm not afraid.

SON: I'm not afraid.

GRANDPA: I have the bat.

DAD: The pitcher has the ball.

SON: And it's just me and the bat and the ball and my day forgotten and my
future not yet born —

GRANDPA: — my best friend about to pitch me his best curveball and me
praying to send it into orbit because that's how you play the game even
in a parking lot in 1947 even when you're a hungry kid and the bat's a
hand-me-down from the other neighborhood's clubhouse —

SON: — and me and the pitcher face each other like two bad guys at high
noon and in slow motion not created by any technology other than my
own God-given eyesight I see his arm wind up and snap the ball clean
to me —

DAD: — and I see it spin on its axis and the smile across my friend's face when
he knows there's no way no how I'm gonna hit it because it's a spit-slick

untouchable pitch but I see it coming toward me and all thoughts scatter like a handful of jacks —

GRANDPA: — and I am the thing in which the angels assemble power and awe and somewhere the round vowels of the church bells somewhere my heart sweats but it's just me and the ball and me and the ball and me closer closer closer till the instant when the muscles known as my arms and the muscles known as my eyes join forces and say Yes —

SON: — and I swing I hit that ball up up and away and we all stop for a moment in time —

DAD: — freeze frame before such a thing as freeze frame and even the ball obliges even the ball knows it is the subject and object of grace and hope —

GRANDPA: — and a perfect example of what a boy can do on any given day when his best friend stands before him and throws the ball and for a minute —

SON: — for a second —

DAD: — the ball stops in its arc and we watch.

GRANDPA: We wait.

SON: And for a while this perfect white ball in this perfect game . . .

DAD: Hangs in the sky held by the hands of clouds.

GRANDPA: It's clean
    and bright
    and pure.

SON: And to us

DAD: it is

GRANDPA: the sun.

(The crack of the bat. Their eyes follow the ball as it sails, as it soars. So high, so far they have to stand. The ball flies up up up till it stops in midflight, high and bright as the noon sun. They can't take their eyes off of it. And they smile the smiles of children.)

END OF PLAY

Bright. Apple. Crush.

STEVEN CHRISTOPHER YOCKEY

Bright. Apple. Crush. was originally produced December 7–10, 2006, by Vital Theatre Company at the McGinn/Cazale Theatre, New York City. Directed by Bob Cline. The cast included: Ethan — Chris Van Hoy, Nancy — Mary Ann Welshans, Dan — Michael Busillo.

CHARACTERS

ETHAN: a man, early twenties, charismatic, loose. He has cigarettes, a lighter, and an easy calmness about him.

NANCY: a woman, early twenties, put together, stoic. She has an apple but guards it from the audience.

DAN: a man, early twenties, quiet, nervous, sweet. He is dressed stylishly and wears a pair of heavy boots. He has a somewhat-healed black eye.

PRODUCTION NOTES

[ ] indicates overlapping dialogue.

Three pools of light spaced evenly across the stage serve as the setting.

If smoking on stage (even limited) is not an available option, Ethan can repeatedly light a cigarette and put it out without taking a drag. Or simply play with a cigarette lighter.

In the overlapping monologues, key moments should rise to prominence. An ebb and flow of the stories. The piece should move as swiftly as possible without glossing over details.

• • •

Light rises to dim, revealing three people standing on stage. Lights up full on Ethan. He is lighting a cigarette. Takes a single drag and immediately puts it out with a smirk.

ETHAN: It's not going to help.

(Lights up full on Nancy. She is polishing a red apple. She looks up and hides it behind her back.)

NANCY: Teaching is not for everyone.

(Lights up full on Dan. He is tying up his left boot. He finishes and stands.)

DAN: Love can make you, I don't know, so you don't think straight.

ETHAN: I should introduce myself. Ethan.

NANCY: I'm Nancy. Nancy Miller. You might have read about me . . .

DAN: My name's Dan.

ETHAN: And I mean I can explain it, absolutely, but it'll only make things [worse.]

NANCY: [Those kids] were horrible. I can't say a single nice thing. And their parents [were just . . .]

DAN: [I never] could put it into words.

NANCY: Some people shouldn't be allowed to have children.

DAN: He was the best thing that ever happened to me.

NANCY: There was one little boy who would kick me as hard as he could. Every chance he got. [I couldn't believe it.]

DAN: [I couldn't believe it] when he asked me out. It was like, like . . .

NANCY: Ridiculously painful. Every day, every time, kicking me. And he was one of the better kids. If that gives you an idea of how bad they really were.

ETHAN: But really, I think if you could have seen the fire. I mean, it might not be your thing, but it was seriously impressive. Seriously. Just an amazing fire. Big and hot, waves of heat, so you couldn't look right at it. You had to look away.

DAN: He is, was the absolute love of my life.

ETHAN: I didn't look away though.

NANCY: It's hard when you decide you're really going to try and help people. Become a teacher; take a job where you can make a difference. Where you think you can make a difference. It's hard when that turns out to be impossible.

DAN: After months of dating, the best kind of dating, the sweet, hot, can't be without them kind of dating, we decided to move in together.

ETHAN: (*He lights another cigarette while speaking and then puts it out again quickly after one drag . . .*) So like I said, I can explain it. She was cheating on me. That afternoon, there was some kind of accident at the local school and they sent everyone home, I mean I usually work most of the night. So I came home early.

DAN: Big decision: to live together. But it felt right.

ETHAN: He was there, in my bed, with my wife, just crazy sex. So they didn't even, I walked in, but they didn't see me. I stood there for a while and they still didn't see me. Because they were so into . . . So I turned around and walked out.

DAN: It wasn't perfect dating, I don't want to sound, you know, it was good. We did have some fights, no big deal. Some of them had even become kind of physical, but it was nothing.

NANCY: That's frustrating. Especially when you can help a kid and they don't want it. Like they know anything. When you're trying to help a kid and they act like they're smarter than you.

DAN: So I asked him to move in and he said yes.

NANCY: A bunch of fucking ten year olds.

ETHAN: I didn't know the guy. I thought maybe I would know him.

NANCY: Like they know anything . . . except how to be mean. No one warns you about that, in college, in your classes. Even when you're assistant teaching, no one tells you. Kids can be terrible.

DAN: The second night after he moved in, I spilled a bottle of wine. It was just careless.

ETHAN: There was rope in the closet at the end of the hall. I could still hear them.

DAN: He hit me so hard that I blacked out, square in the jaw. Just a sharp pain and then nothing. When I woke up, he was asleep. I wasn't even sure it even . . . And then I cleaned up the wine.

NANCY: I remember so vividly the moment when I just snapped.

DAN: That started to happen a lot. Not the spilling . . .

NANCY: I was at my desk.

DAN: The hitting.

NANCY: I was trying to explain photosynthesis. Well, the way you explain photosynthesis to a bunch of ten year olds.
(*In her condescending teacher's voice . . .*) "The plants have their leaves and the sunlight shines down, [bright light . . . "]

DAN: [Bright light] shining in through the curtains. My apartment faced these security lights. It never really got dark. And he hadn't noticed until he moved in, so this became another source of tension. Something that was my fault.

NANCY: And as I'm trying to teach these kids something, I'm writing on the board, with my back to them like this . . .
(*She turns and speaks over her shoulder.*)
And I get hit with something, hit hard in the shoulder and then again in the leg. And again in the hip.

DAN: It got so the bruises were becoming something I had to explain. I felt like a bad after-school special. But then, it seemed like most of the stuff actually could have been avoided, if I had just paid more attention.

NANCY: It took me a moment to even realize what was happening. They were throwing rocks at me. These kids in my class, these young kids, were actually throwing rocks at me. [And laughing.]

ETHAN: [And laughing,] they were laughing and grunting and all of the sudden it sounded like I was in a tunnel, with traffic, this roaring white noise that kind of shoved everything else into the background. And I realized I was squeezing the rope so tight that my hands were raw.

DAN: And that was OK for a while. He was the first person I ever loved, he was the first guy I ever had sex with, and really good sex. He was everything. And you take the good with the bad. That's how it works.

NANCY: I couldn't even speak.

ETHAN: (*He lights another cigarette, takes a single drag, looks at it while speaking, and then puts out the cigarette.*) They were still having sex when I hit the guy in the back of the head. I don't even remember really what I hit him with. It was heavy. She screamed out, but it was muddled by the noise in my ears. After I hit her a couple of times, she stopped moving.

DAN: Eventually I got to the point where I stopped flinching. Didn't even try to avoid it. And he seemed to understand. I just accepted it . . .

NANCY: They were hitting [me.]

DAN: [While] he was hitting [me.]

ETHAN: [Eventually] I stopped hitting them. And tied them to the bed.

NANCY: I took the rest of the day off. I went [home.]

DAN: [And] then last night something was [different.]

ETHAN: [And] I walked [downstairs.]

DAN: [And] I didn't feel anything at all when he hit [me.]

ETHAN: [And] I walked [outside.]

DAN: [And] I didn't fall [down.]

ETHAN: [And] I walked to the [garage.]

DAN: [And] I was aware on some level that my body was moving, but it was like watching a movie, you know? But standing right up against the screen, so the images don't make sense.

NANCY: (*She pulls the apple from behind her back where she has been hiding it in one hand or the other.*) While I was at home, I had some time to think. To really think about what happened, about everything that had happened in my three months at that school. I made some decisions. About those fucking ten years olds.

(*Ethan lights a cigarette, looks at it, puts it out without taking a drag.*)

If you can't teach them to even be human, then what good are they?

DAN: It's all kind of a blur still.

ETHAN: The garage is where we kept the gasoline.

NANCY: (*She handles the apple.*) And then it was clear. And really [simple . . .]

ETHAN: [It was] really [simple.]

DAN: [It seemed] so . . . simple. I just, I looked down and somehow he was on the floor. And there was blood. And I kept bringing my boot down on his neck and face. I remember thinking that it shouldn't be happening, but not having any control over it. There was a point where I didn't even recognize him anymore and my boot was covered in blood.

(He looks at his boot.)

NANCY: *(She tosses and catches the apple.)* The healthiest snack in the world.

ETHAN: *(He lights the lighter once or twice.)* I always carry a lighter.

DAN: All of the sudden I could hear my breathing and my heart slamming in my chest, tears on my face, wet and sticky. But I still didn't stop.

ETHAN: Just like this . . .

(He lights a cigarette, takes a single drag, holds out his lighter, lights it, and leans forward as if setting something on fire. He then backs away, exhaling the smoke while saying . . .)

And whoosh!

NANCY: I passed them out and said: *(A return to the teacher's voice .)* "All right, it's important that you all stay healthy. But I know not everyone loves to eat apples. So here's a little deal for you guys: Whoever finishes their apple first will get an extra twenty minutes at recess."

DAN: It all happened [so quickly.]

ETHAN: [It all happened] [so quickly.]

NANCY: [It all happened] so quickly. They just started tearing into the apples. And I'll confess that [it was exciting.]

DAN: [It was exciting] and horrifying all at once. [It was a rush.]

ETHAN: [It was a rush] of flame up the side of the building. Faster than I would have imagined.

NANCY: I didn't expect them all to react with such enthusiasm for just twenty extra minutes at recess. I thought it would somehow be harder.

DAN: I finally stopped.

NANCY: I might have used too much poison.

ETHAN: I'm sure they woke up at some point.

NANCY: If I had known they'd be so voracious, I probably would have eased off a bit.

DAN: I was covered in blood.

NANCY: I like to think I would have been more restrained.

ETHAN: I like to think they woke up, right in the middle of it.

DAN: You never think of yourself as . . .

NANCY: But that might be too generous really.

DAN: When it was over, I didn't really know what to do. I took off my boots; I didn't want to be in them. I didn't think, I don't, I just took them off. And he was laying there kind of moving some, so I took my clothes off, [put them in the washing machine and went, naked, back into the living room. He was still moving. I picked up my boots and took them to the bathtub. I let it fill up while I sat in the tub scrubbing the boots.

After just a few minutes, the water was red and soapy, but the boots were clean. Wet and clean. I drained the tub, took a shower, cleaned it with bleach. I dried myself off, moved my clothes from the washer to the dryer, threw in the boots and walked back into the living room. He was still moving a little, breathing through, trying to breath. I watched him while I waited for the dryer to finish. At one point he reached towards me and I started to sob uncontrollably. When my clothes were dry, I got dressed again, even the boots. And I called the police and asked for an ambulance.]

NANCY: [It took about ten minutes before the first one started convulsing. But it happened quickly after that. I wouldn't let any of them go to the bathroom, I wouldn't let any of them leave. I told them to stay in their seats and for the first time, and I don't know if they were afraid or disoriented or just stunned, but they did as they were told. [I sat behind my desk and watched these horrible children drop to the floor or collapse onto their own desks one by one in pools of spit and some crimson streaks. And they were crying and asking for help and confused. Clearly confused. It's hard for me to say this, but honestly it was a real delight to see these worthless children suffer the way that I had suffered when all I wanted to do was help them become better people. There were only one or two left mildly conscious when I even began to realize that this might cause a problem.]

ETHAN: [I watched the fire, stood really close to it. I watched it for a while. When the roof caved in, this billow of smoke was released all at once; this thick, dark smoke and I had to move back a good bit because I was coughing so much. I didn't really think of anything, but I got in my car to drive away. And I couldn't, I couldn't make myself leave. Instead I just backed up and kept watching the house the burn. I needed to watch it for as long as I could. When I heard the sirens from the fire trucks, then I drove away.]

(Pause. Nancy takes a bite of the apple. The other two men look at her as she chews and swallows. They all look out again . . .)

NANCY: I knew they wouldn't understand. No one. So the general reaction didn't surprise me. Maybe some of the other teachers, but no, no one did.

DAN: I feel like I could hear the sirens for hours before anyone actually got there. I just stayed on the couch, far away from him.

NANCY: But I think the other teachers were secretly proud of me.

DAN: It took forever, but I could hear the sirens. They said, they told me that there was a huge fire a few blocks down. Those were the sirens. That they were sorry it took so long for the ambulance to . . .

ETHAN: When they spoke to me, the police told me that they had assumed I was the man in bed with my wife.

DAN: I told them I came home from drinks with friends and found him like that.

ETHAN: So they were surprised.

NANCY: I don't even read the papers or watch television anymore, because of the ridiculous things people are saying about me.

DAN: I rode with him in the ambulance to the hospital, I held his hand, and waited while he was in surgery.

ETHAN: There's going to be an investigation. I suppose that makes sense.

NANCY: Saying I hate children. It's amazing what people will believe.

DAN: I don't know what I'll do when he wakes up. When he can tell people what happened. What I, what I did . . . to him.

ETHAN: I didn't really try to cover anything up. I wasn't thinking that way I guess. I wasn't thinking [at all . . .]

NANCY: [Listen,] I took that job because I love kids.

ETHAN: And I'm still sure they deserved it. I feel it in my bones.

NANCY: Those weren't kids though, you see? They were . . . something else.

DAN: I sit alone now and [wait.]

NANCY: [I've been] told, as part of the whole court thing, that I'll be going to a hospital. Where someone will take care of me for a change.

DAN: I sit by his hospital bed and think about what he might say when he wakes up, if he'd remember it at all. I barely do.

ETHAN: That doesn't make it better.

NANCY: That will be nice. Healthy. Or, I don't know . . .

DAN: But the doctors, due to the extent of his injuries, they don't think he'll wake up.

ETHAN: (*Lights a cigarette, takes a single drag . . . *) I just, I wish I could describe the fire to you, [it was . . .]

NANCY: [It doesn't] matter anyway. No harm [done.]

DAN: [But the thing] I remember most . . .

ETHAN: (*He lights the lighter, cigarette hanging from his lips .*) Bright.

NANCY: (*She holds out the apple.*) Apple?

DAN: (*Stomps his boot down once, loudly [and for the only time].*) . . . Crush. (*Blackout.*)

END OF PLAY

Charm

FREDERICK STROPPEL

Charm was originally staged at the Theatre Artists Workshop in Norwalk, Conn. It was directed by the author and had the following cast: Leona — Nadine Willig, Melvin — James Noble, Sam — Drew Denbaum.

CHARACTERS

    LEONA: a middle-aged suburban housewife, just a bit spacey and clueless

    MELVIN: Leona's husband; gruff, cranky, and too long tolerant of his
        wife's carefree ways

    SAM: a mysterious stranger

SETTING

    A suburban living room

• • •

*A living room. Melvin sits in front of the TV. His wife Leona enters through
the front door, somewhat harried.*

LEONA: Melvin. Melvin. I need some cash. I have to pay the cabbie.

MELVIN: *(Befuddled.)* Cash . . . ?

    (Pulls out his wallet.)

    All right, how much . . . ?

LEONA: *(Grabs money.)* Just give me the ten.

MELVIN: But where's the . . . ?

    (Leona exits. Melvin goes to the window, looks out. Leona returns.)

LEONA: Whew! What a day!

MELVIN: Leona — where's the car?

LEONA: The car? Oh, I lost the car.

MELVIN: You lost the car?

LEONA: That's why I took a cab, silly.

MELVIN: Where did you lose it? In the parking lot?

LEONA: I didn't *lose it*, lose it. It's just gone.

MELVIN: It's gone? Someone stole it? Did you call the police?

LEONA: What are the police going to do? I signed it over, fair and square, it's
    all legal.

MELVIN: You signed it over? You *sold* the car?

LEONA: No, I didn't *sell* it. My stars, you're dense today. It's just *gone*. Sam's
    got it.

MELVIN: Sam? Who's Sam?

LEONA: Who's Sam?

    (Wistful.)

    Sam is a very charming man. I spent an exceedingly pleasant afternoon
    with Sam.

MELVIN: *(Jealousy rising.)* You spent the afternoon with some fellow named Sam? Doing *what?*

LEONA: Oh, please. It was all innocent and aboveboard; he didn't lay a finger on me. And yet, in another, finer sense, he touched me to the deepest recesses of my being. *(Sighs.)*

MELVIN: Leona, you know I give you a pretty loose rein when it comes to handling the household affairs, but this whole Sam thing seems a little dicey, and I'm going to have to insist that you explain it to me.

LEONA: I suppose I must. Well, I was at Shop-Rite, and in the deli section there was a man giving out samples of deviled ham on a cracker. Well, you know, I have never been a strong exponent of deviled ham, or any meat spreads for that matter, but this salesman had such a winning smile, and he imparted such a sense of trust, that I threw caution to the winds and took a bite. And you know, it was mouth-wateringly good. I bought six cans.

(Holds up the bag.)

MELVIN: Six cans? That's a bit extravagant, don't you think?

LEONA: He also sold me a little cheese-board set, and a case of horseradish sauce.

MELVIN: This was the Sam fellow?

LEONA: *(Nods.)* Now you know I'm a prudent and scientific shopper, but the way he spoke to me, the personal interest he showed, the certainty in his mind that each one of these items would make a welcome addition to my lifestyle — I just couldn't say no.

MELVIN: A *case* of horseradish sauce?

LEONA: Then we started chatting in a low-key amiable fashion, and I found him utterly charming. So much so, that when he suggested going for coffee, the notion seemed irresistible to me. And there was a Starbucks right on the corner, and I know how you absolutely refuse to go in there —

MELVIN: Pay three dollars for a cup of coffee? Not in my lifetime.

LEONA: — so it seemed to me that this might be my only chance to experience this unique cultural phenomenon.

(Giggles.) I had a frappucino.

MELVIN: And this fellow just left his deviled-ham stand, flat?

LEONA: Well — in retrospect, I don't think he was working for Hormel at all. I think he used that as an opening to get to me.

MELVIN: *(Knowingly.)* To *get* to you? Aha.

LEONA: Stop being so dirty-minded — honestly, Melvin, your brain is marinated in sewage. He wanted to *talk* to me, that's all, he wanted to connect with me. And when he flashed that smile, that charming smile — well, I just melted into a puddle, that's a fact. We talked about our lives, and our families, and our dreams and so forth . . . *(Grimly.)* Then he walked me back to my car, and that's when it happened.

MELVIN: It?

LEONA: He really admired our Camry, and told me he'd always wanted one himself, and he asked me if I would give it to him. And I don't know, it might have been the afternoon heat or the sugar in the frappucino, but I said sure, take it.

MELVIN: You said take it?

LEONA: I said take it.

MELVIN: And he took it?

LEONA: Yes.

MELVIN: Hmm. You know what I think? I think this man's a professional charmer. He's one of those fellows who goes from town to town, charming weak impressionable women.

LEONA: I'm afraid I do lack a certain spine in my character.

MELVIN: Oh, he struck the mother lode with you. I'm surprised he stopped at the car.

LEONA: He didn't.

MELVIN: *(A sinking feeling.)* He didn't?

LEONA: *(Sighs.)* You might as well know, Melvin — everything's gone. The house, the bank accounts, my wallet . . . *everything.*

MELVIN: You gave him *everything?*

LEONA: He asked. I gave.

MELVIN: But . . . you can't give things away that easily. You need contracts.

LEONA: Oh, he had contracts. His pockets were full of contracts. I kept signing, and signing, and signing. He had to guide my hand after a while, it was starting to cramp.

MELVIN: That doesn't mean any of it's legal. Were there witnesses?

LEONA: We didn't need any. He's a Notary.

MELVIN: Jesus, Leona, you are such an almighty twit. Just had to go to Starbucks, when I've warned you time and time again . . . ! Fucking frappucinos . . . !

LEONA: He *charmed* me, Melvin. Charm is a wonderful, dangerous thing. If you have charm, you can enchant the world. I have no charm. Neither have you. We are two charmless people, and see where it's gotten us.

MELVIN: *(Disagreeing.)* I think *I* have a modicum of charm.

LEONA: No, you don't, dear. You have solidity, consistency, and adequate earning power. But no charm. I think that's why I married you. I found your lack of sparkle oddly comforting.

MELVIN: *(Goes to the phone.)* Well, I may not have charm or sparkle, but I have a lawyer. And he'll take care of this flim-flam artist quick enough . . .

LEONA: It's too late, Melvin. He took my blood. The bargain is sealed.

MELVIN: He took your blood?

LEONA: Yes, but so smoothly, so skillfully, I didn't feel a thing.

MELVIN: He made you sign in blood?

LEONA: Only the last contract. The one for my soul.

MELVIN: Oh, for Christ's sake! You sold him your soul? Now that was pretty damned stupid! Why, this fellow must have been Satan himself! Didn't you realize?

LEONA: I realize now. Although I don't think he's the actual Satan. Probably one of his many emissaries.

MELVIN: Deviled ham . . . ! That should have been the tip-off right there! My God, you always manage to cozy up to the biggest leeches! Your brother wasn't bad enough . . . !

LEONA: Look, I'm not happy about it, either. But what's done is done. What do I need a soul for, anyway? It's not like I ever use it.

MELVIN: I don't know about your soul, Leona, but the house is in both our names, and if this character thinks he's moving in here and sitting in my La-Z-Boy he's gonna have to deal with me.

LEONA: *(Nods.)* He knows. He'll be here any minute. He wanted to get the car washed first.

MELVIN: He's coming here? All right, what do we need?
(Rummaging around.)
Garlic, and a crucifix, and silver bullets . . . I suppose we're all out of holy water?
(Melvin exits into kitchen.)

LEONA: It won't do you any good, Melvin. Once he flashes that smile and suckers you in, there's no hope. No hope!
(Knock on the door. Melvin returns to answer it.)

LEONA: Don't look him in the eye, whatever you do.

MELVIN: Let me handle this, woman. *(Grumbles.)* By God, I'm tired of cleaning up after your messes . . .
(Melvin opens the door. Sam walks in.)

SAM: *(Charmingly.)* Hello! I'm Sam.

MELVIN: *(Momentarily stunned by his charm.)* Uh . . . Hi.

SAM: You must be Melvin.

MELVIN: Well . . . Yes.

(Sam shakes his hand.)

SAM: You've got a nice strong handshake there, Melvin.

MELVIN: Thank you.

SAM: And this is your house. You must be very proud.

MELVIN: I suppose . . .

SAM: Leona tells me you built that porch deck all by yourself. I'm impressed.

MELVIN: Nothing, really . . .

SAM: Oh, come, come. I can see that you're a man of style and accomplishment, and uncommon grace.

MELVIN: *(Pleased.)* Well . . . *(Clears his throat.)* Listen, Sam . . . These contracts . . . My wife . . .

SAM: Yes?

MELVIN: *(Looking away.)* Uh . . . it's just not . . . I don't think . . . we just won't . . .

SAM: Melvin, am I wrong, or are you averting your gaze from me?

MELVIN: No, it's just . . . I have a lazy eye . . .

SAM: *(Coaxing him.)* Melvin? Mel-vin . . . .

(Melvin slowly looks up at Sam. Sam cracks a wide smile.)

MELVIN: Oh, Jesus . . . ! Leona, he's smiling at me!

LEONA: Look away!

MELVIN: I can't! He's charming!

SAM: I understand you have quite the burgeoning stock portfolio.

MELVIN: *(Falling under his spell.)* Yes . . . Yes, I do.

SAM: And a sturdy 401(k) plan?

LEONA: Be strong, Melvin! Be strong!

SAM: *(Turning his smile on Leona.)* Did you say something, Leona?

LEONA: *(Melting.)* Why, no, Sam. Not a thing.

MELVIN: *(Spellbound.)* Yes, I have many assets at my disposal, Sam.

SAM: Including several children, I understand?

MELVIN: And a grandchild on the way.

SAM: Isn't that great? What do you say we step out and get some coffee? I know a charming little spot.

MELVIN: Sounds terrific.

SAM: I'll drive.

(Sam and Melvin exit. Leona rushes to the door.)

LEONA: *(Calls after him.)* Melvin! Try the frappucino!

END OF PLAY

The Great Helmsman

DAVID HENRY HWANG

The Great Helmsman was first presented by Second Generation (Gladys Chen, President) as part of *Ten* at the Joseph Papp Public Theater (Newman Theater) on April 30, 2007. Produced and directed by Lloyd Suh, with the following cast:
Ai — Jessica Jade Andres, Mei — Allison Mui,
Kang — Yung-I Chang.

CHARACTERS

   AI: Asian woman, late teens

   MEI: Asian woman, late teens

   KANG: Asian, either gender, any age

SETTING

   The Forbidden City, Beijing, China, 1969

•   •   •

Beijing, the Forbidden City. 1969. Ai and Mei, two girls in their late-teens, sit in a room, empty except for a photo of Chairman Mao and two chairs. Silence.

AI: Respectfully wish Chairman Mao eternal life!
   (Pause.)

MEI: The hearts of the sons and daughters of Yennan go out to Chairman Mao!
   (Pause.)

AI: Advance victoriously while following Chairman Mao's revolutionary line in literature and the arts.
   (Pause.)

MEI: In agriculture, learn from Danzai!
   (Ai snorts derisively.)

MEI: What.

AI: That is so old.

MEI: No.

AI: That slogan was around when my mother was a girl.

MEI: It is still highly relevant!

AI: All right.

MEI: The agricultural accomplishments of Danzai continue to lead the nation.

AI: Have it your way.

MEI: Perhaps you are not aware, Comrade, of the latest production statistics for barley and —

AI: Yadda, yadda, yadda.

MEI: — and rice and — What is this, "yadda, yadda, yadda"?

AI: I'm not saying Danzai isn't still a model for all workers and peasants.

MEI: Well, then —

AI: All I'm saying is that your slogan is old!

MEI: And old is bad?

AI: Not necessarily.

MEI: Then why are you even — ?

AI: Of course, we must destroy the Four Olds.

MEI: Yes, of course! Old ideas! Old culture! Old customs! Old habits!

AI: Well, then —

MEI: But Danzai is not old!

AI: But your slogan is.

MEI: It is still perfectly relevant!

AI: Fine. You go in there and start spouting off about Danzai. You'll see what happens.

    (Pause.)

MEI: I don't believe you. The Chairman is still very committed to promoting the ideal of Danzai as a glorious example to soldiers and peasants throughout the Great Proletarian State.

AI: You sure about that?

MEI: Why wouldn't — ?

AI: Did he tell you that himself?

MEI: No, but —

AI: I see.

MEI: Did he tell you something different?

AI: What happened between the Chairman and me is for him to disclose. I'm just saying, Comrade, you should really try to stay up-to-date. Come up with a more current slogan. Otherwise — well, it makes you look old.

MEI: Do I look old?

AI: I'm just engaging in constructive criticism.

MEI: Last time I saw the Chairman, he told me I looked young.

AI: "Last time." Like you've visited him so many times?

MEI: Well, no, but —

AI: That's what I thought.

MEI: He told me that my cheeks were as fresh as the peaches grown in Sichuan.

AI: What makes you so sure he likes peaches?

MEI: He does, doesn't he?

AI: Have you ever seen him eat one?

MEI: Who doesn't like peaches? Everyone loves peaches!

AI: Not everyone!

MEI: Yes, everyone! They are a Great Proletarian Fruit!

AI: Still, they figure into many legends which promote old thinking and feudal oppression.

MEI: That is the fault of the legends, not the fruit!

AI: OK.

MEI: The Chairman compared my cheeks to peaches, so peaches must be good.

AI: Unless they're part of the Four Olds, in which case he was trying to tell you that you're maybe looking a little tired.

MEI: He kissed my cheeks!

AI: Is that all?

MEI: No.

AI: Then what — ?

MEI: That is none of your business!

AI: Really, I don't even know why I'm trying to help you, Comrade.

MEI: The Chairman and I —

AI: After all, you're not going to be the one who sees him tonight, anyway.

MEI: Of course I am — I mean, if the Chairman so chooses.

AI: But he won't.

MEI: Oh — you think he'll choose you?

AI: I know what he likes.

MEI: What makes you so certain?

AI: It's easy to tell — from the sounds of his moans.

MEI: Well!

AI: Let's just say that I showed our Chairman the true fervor of Revolutionary youth.

MEI: For your information, he did not only kiss my cheeks!

AI: What then?

MEI: First he kissed my cheeks, then my lips, then he put his hands on me, and then —

AI: Yes?

MEI: We struggled.

AI: Well, he didn't have to struggle much with me.

MEI: Struggle is glorious!

AI: Struggling against the Four Olds is glorious. Struggling against the Chairman — eeenh.

MEI: I did not struggle against the Chairman, I struggled with him! Together, we struggled — inside me!

AI: Well, in my case, he didn't have to struggle, he just slipped right in.

MEI: That is the same thing —

AI: Of course, it might've not gone so easily with you — you and your old slogans.

MEI: What are you — ?

AI: With age, women tend to get . . . dryer.

MEI: I was fully lubricated! The moment he touched me. I was wet like the — like the hot springs at Chengdu!

AI: Excuse me?

MEI: I mean, like the —

AI: Chengdu? There are no hot springs at Chengdu!

MEI: Guiyang! I meant, like the hot springs at —

AI: You made that up, didn't you?

MEI: No, I —

AI: Admit it, you made up a slogan!

MEI: No, I just forgot the city, that's all.

AI: There is no revolutionary slogan that involves hot springs.

MEI: Yes, there is. It's just not — very well-known, that's all.

AI: Why? Because it was invented — by rightists?

MEI: Of course not!

AI: Confess! Engage in self-criticism!

MEI: Please, I was just —

AI: Wait until Comrade Kang hears about this.

MEI: Kang? No!

AI: You think — you think he'll ever allow you in there again?

MEI: Please, Comrade Ai —

AI: A youth who subverts the wisdom of the Great Proletarian State?

MEI: It was just a slip of the tongue!

AI: No, the choice is clear. You lack revolutionary purity! You're not the one who will be visiting the Chairman tonight! It will be me!
     (Pause.)
     I won, I won, I won! I can feel the Great Helmsman in my mouth already!

MEI: He will forgive me.

AI: Kang will never —

MEI: No, not Kang!

AI: Then who?

MEI: The Chairman himself.

AI: You will not even get to see the Chairman tonight.

MEI: Yes, I will.

AI: Now, you are filled with counter-revolutionary delusions.

MEI: Just wait and see.

AI: Fine. Why don't we call Kang right now and ask him?

> *(Pause.)*
>
> Did you hear me? I said, I'm going to call Kang.
>
> *(Pause.)*
>
> What's wrong with you? Have you been brainwashed by the filthy landowners and the cowardly capitalists?
>
> *(Pause.)*
>
> Say something! What do you know that I don't?

MEI: Kang heard.

AI: Heard what?

MEI: He heard the Chairman — struggling with me. I saw Kang — at the window, watching us.

AI: So? Comrade Kang was afraid that your rightist subversion might —

MEI: No. He heard what the Chairman said to me. And he knows the Glorious Leader wants to see me again.

AI: Even though you make up false slogans to mislead the workers?

MEI: It won't make any difference.

AI: You — you're lying — like the paper tiger of — like the final stages of capitalist decline to — like Marxist-Leninist thought will lead to the overthrow of . . .

> *(Pause.)*
>
> What did the Chairman say to you, anyway?!
>
> *(Pause.)*

MEI: Yes, I have seen the Chairman only one time before. But that fact works in my favor, not yours. True, it would be even better if I'd never before been granted a visit. Because the Chairman enjoys bringing inspiration to — fresh youths. But, in my case, I know he will be eager to see me at least once more.

> *(Pause.)*
>
> The Chairman told me he had been visited by hundreds of revolutionary women. But that I was — the most revolutionary of all.

AI: You're lying. How could you — you, who still rattles on about agriculture in Danzai — ?

MEI: He told me that I had the most revolutionary — ass.

> *(Pause.)*
>
> That is why he did not "slip right up" inside me. Why it took us longer — to struggle.
>
> *(Pause.)*

AI: He could've struggled with my ass!

MEI: But he didn't, did he?

AI: All he had to do was ask! Why didn't he ask me? I would gladly have given my ass to promote revolution and production!

MEI: He didn't have to ask me. I offered. In the spirit of a true Marxist-Leninist warrior.

(Pause.)

And inspired by agriculture in Danzai.

(Pause.)

So go on. Tell Kang. Tell him anything you want. It will do you no good. I know — I have already been the one chosen for tonight. I was just trying to help you, Comrade. To perfect your fervor, following the vigorous example of the Ninth Party Congress.

(Kang enters.)

AI: Comrade Kang!

MEI: Comrade Kang!

(Pause.)

AI: Well?

MEI: Who has the Great Helmsman chosen tonight to inspire through his revolutionary example?

AI: Well? Who? Comrade? Who?

KANG: Both. He wants you both. Now — prepare to meet him.

(Kang exits. Silence.)

MEI: Well, it is good, Comrade, that we engaged in this criticism session.

AI: Yes. I feel we have made great strides forward — together.

MEI: Like soldiers, going together into battle —

AI: To fight Soviet hegemony —

MEI: And capitalist exploitation of the working class.

(They begin to undress each other.)

AI: Warriors love reading Chairman Mao's books the most.

MEI: The sunlight of Mao Zedong thought illuminates the road of the Great Proletarian Cultural Revolution.

AI: Forge ahead courageously following the great example of our leader, Chairman Mao.

MEI: Chairman Mao is heir to the 3,000-year-old emperor worship tradition.

AI: Eternal life to Chairman Mao.

MEI: Vigorously serve the Great Helmsman.

(Fade to black. Curtain.)

END OF PLAY

Healing

GUY FREDRICK GLASS

First performed on February 21, 2007 in
the Hackensack Theater and Playwright Festival,
The Hackensack Cultural Arts Center, Hackensack, N.J.
The cast was as follows: Anne — Nanci Cone, Emily —
Hannah Snyder-Beck, Victoria — Jennifer Sandella. Director:
Sara Lampert Hoover; producer: Ciona Taylor Productions.

CHARACTERS
ANNE: a woman in her forties
EMILY: a woman in her thirties
VICTORIA: a woman in her twenties

SETTING
Anne's apartment

TIME
The present

•   •   •

Lights come up on a simply furnished apartment. A couch, a chair, and a coffee table are in the foreground. There is a small kitchen in the background, and a door. Emily and Anne are standing center stage, Emily has just entered the apartment.

EMILY: Am I the first one here?
ANNE: You're the first one. There's another one on the way.
EMILY: Only one?
ANNE: That's all I could get this time. Someone new.
EMILY: Does she know?
ANNE: *(Shaking her head.)* She doesn't suspect a thing. But I think she'll fit in just fine.
EMILY: And the supplies?
ANNE: They're in the other room. In a box. Do you want me to bring it in here?
EMILY: Sometimes it takes a while to explain it to the new ones. Why don't you leave it in there for now. We can get it out later.
ANNE: Do you want something to drink?
EMILY: I'll take anything cold. The colder the better.
ANNE: We've got Diet Dr. Pepper.
EMILY: Perfect.
ANNE: With or without caffeine? *(Beat.)* I've got both.
    (Anne walks over to the kitchen.)
EMILY: Surprise me. I like to live dangerously.
ANNE: *(Pouring soda.)* It's been a while, hasn't it?

EMILY: Too long. You know, I can't live without my occasional "fix." I find myself thinking about my visits to you at the weirdest times.

(Anne returns, with two glasses of soda in her hands.)

ANNE: It's hard to go without for so long. I know the feeling.

(Anne hands a glass to Emily.)

EMILY: I guess we all have our vices. And ours is pretty harmless, in the greater scheme of things.

(They clink glasses.)

ANNE: At least we're not hurting anybody but ourselves.

EMILY: And nobody else has to know about it.

(They drink. Doorbell.)

ANNE: Oops. There she is. The new person. *(Shouting.)* Come in, the door's open.

VICTORIA: *(Entering.)* You leave your door unlocked? I'm so paranoid. How do you know I'm not an ax murderer?

ANNE: I'm Anne. This is Emily.

EMILY: *(Smiling.)* I'm the ax murderer.

VICTORIA: I'm Victoria. Never Vickie. Always Victoria.

EMILY: That's a beautiful name.

VICTORIA: My mother thought it was elegant. It's the only beautiful thing she ever gave me.

EMILY: That's sad.

VICTORIA: People hear it and they think I'm rich or something. But I just work in a health food store.

ANNE: So, can I get you some healthy liquid chemicals? We're drinking Diet Dr. Pepper.

VICTORIA: That'll corrode your insides. Unless you have soy milk, I'll pass . . . I didn't really expect to get a meal or anything when I answered the ad in the personals.

EMILY: What did you expect?

(Anne beckons them to sit. Victoria sits on the chair, Anne and Emily sit on the couch together.)

VICTORIA: *(Taking out a crumpled piece of newspaper from her pocket.)* What would you expect? *(Reading.)* "Wanted, young women with a sense of adventure, to share nonsexual peak experiences with other like-minded women." And then a phone number.

ANNE: My phone number.

VICTORIA: Yes. To tell you the truth, all kinds of wild fantasies have gone through my head. The soda's not part of the deal, is it? I don't like drinks with chemicals.

ANNE: No. The Diet Dr. Pepper is purely optional. *(To Emily.)* Shall I get it out of the other room now, Emily? Shall I bring in the box?

EMILY: No, not yet.

VICTORIA: What's in the box?

EMILY: Never mind. You're not ready for it yet. You're not ready for what's in the box.

VICTORIA: *(Eagerly.)* When will I be ready? Is it part of the peak experience?

ANNE: It is the peak experience. It's the experience you've been waiting for your whole life.

VICTORIA: Now you've got me really curious. How big is this box? Is it bigger than a breadbox?

ANNE: No. It's smaller than a breadbox. It's just a cardboard box that my Nikes came in. I save the boxes from my sneakers. They're just the right size.

VICTORIA: The right size for what? What's inside of it?

EMILY: You have to be worthy of what's inside the box.

VICTORIA: I answered the ad. It didn't say anything about that.

ANNE: You answered an ad. You called me. You knocked on the door. So what? Why should we share what's in the box with you, just like that?

EMILY: We don't know you.

ANNE: You have to show us that you're worthy.

EMILY: That you're one of us.

ANNE: That what's inside the box will mean as much to you as it does to us.

VICTORIA: How can I do that if I don't know what's inside?

EMILY: We can get a pretty good idea by spending some time with you. A pretty good idea of how much you'll appreciate what we have to give . . . What would you like there to be in the box?

VICTORIA: I would like there not to be drugs in the box.

ANNE: *(Laughing.)* Drugs? We're not about that at all. You can be sure there are no drugs in the box.

EMILY: Anything else? Be creative. Think.

VICTORIA: I would like there to be something in the box that makes me feel like myself, only better. Something that makes me feel clearer than clear and more real than real.

ANNE: You're on the right track.

EMILY: Do you ever feel like you're missing something, Victoria? Like you're missing an ingredient that other people have?

VICTORIA: *(Quietly.)* Yes.

EMILY: We all did, until we found what's in the box.

ANNE: *(Tenderly.)* Until we found each other.

EMILY: I got married once. Feels like a whole lifetime ago. Married at the age of eighteen to the only man I ever dated.

VICTORIA: Were you pregnant? Is that why you married him?

EMILY: You ask a lot of questions. No I wasn't pregnant then, but I got pregnant later. I don't know why I married him. Really I was bored. That's the story of my life. I was bored and I thought getting married would make me feel unbored.

VICTORIA: And?

EMILY: I was bored because I've got something missing inside of me. That's what I discovered later, after I made a lot of mistakes. In the meantime, I tried every way I could think of to get rid of the bored feeling. My husband worked long hours. I was at home alone. I had a baby because I wanted a companion, a playmate. You know, for all the wrong reasons. We turned the guest room into a nursery. That took a few months, kept me busy. I thought the bored feeling had gone away forever. But I was wrong.

VICTORIA: What happened?

EMILY: A month after the baby was born, the excitement died down, then I was left with this tiny, noisy creature that needed attention all the time. It took away the little bit of attention I got from my husband, and I was more bored than ever. Bored and hopeless. Then I answered Anne's ad and my world changed.

ANNE: I was married too. But that was a long long time ago. My husband used to beat me when he was drunk. I still have some of the scars on my back. Now, I don't even remember what he looked like. The only reminder of our relationship is those scars.

VICTORIA: That's awful.

ANNE: It doesn't bother me anymore. I can't even see the scars. And even then, I learned that there was a way to distance myself emotionally from what was happening to me physically. At first I tried to do it all inside my head. I even bought a book on self-hypnosis. Then when the beatings came, I would just try to telescope myself into my own personal world, and the pain seemed to be happening to somebody else.

VICTORIA: Did it work?

ANNE: It worked for a while. But then one day I was experimenting and I came up with a better way to liberate myself from the pain.

EMILY: Thank God.

ANNE: And it did more than liberate me from the pain. It made me feel wonderful for the first time . . . And the first thing I decided to do, after I put my life back together, was to give of myself to others. So that others would never have to go through the pain I had gone through. And so that others could share in what I had learned, in what I had to learn for myself.

VICTORIA: And what did you learn?

EMILY: Ah, now you're trying to figure out what's in the box.

ANNE: We have to feel safe sharing our secret with you.

EMILY: We have to know that you've suffered in some way, like we have.

ANNE: And that you can benefit from what's inside.

VICTORIA: Well, I've never been married, and no one has ever abused me. But it's not like I'm happy. I mean, I'm actually really unhappy.

ANNE: We were all unhappy, once.

(Anne puts her hand on Victoria's hand.)

VICTORIA: My father disappeared before I was born. My mother used to lie in bed and cry and cry and cry. She didn't pay attention to whether I went to school or not. Everything centered around her needs. I just didn't count. I never felt any good about myself. I felt like I wanted to shrink into nothingness. That's when I started to starve myself. So that I could really shrink away to nothing. I got so I was so thin I had to be taken away.

EMILY: I see.

VICTORIA: Somehow I managed to get myself functioning, at least on the surface. Years of therapy. Hospitalizations and rehospitalizations. Now I'm at a normal weight, more or less. I still have to force myself to eat. Working in a health food store helps me to keep track of what I put in my mouth and to make sure I don't end up back in the hospital.

ANNE: And why did you answer my ad?

VICTORIA: It's kind of hard to explain, but the truth is I got a kind of thrill from starving myself that nothing else matches. When you haven't eaten for a few days you feel ill, at first. Then a kind of rush sets in. Then the longer you starve yourself, the higher you feel. I've never been able to duplicate that feeling. I'm always looking for that peak experience. I don't know what I expected to find here. Maybe I've come to the wrong place.

EMILY: I think you may have come to the right place.

VICTORIA: Can I know what's in the box now? Can I see what it is?

ANNE: *(To Emily.)* Do you think she's ready for it, Emily?

EMILY: *(Shaking her head.)* Yes. You can get the box now, Anne.
(Anne gets up and walks offstage. She brings back a box and places it on the coffee table, and sits down again.)

EMILY: *(To Victoria.)* Open the box.
(Victoria opens the box. She takes out three razor blades which she holds cautiously in her palms.)

VICTORIA: These are razor blades. One says Emily. One says Anne. And one says Victoria.

ANNE: Yes. We've been waiting for you.

VICTORIA: *(Mesmerized.)* Look at how shiny they are. *(Frightened, Victoria drops the blades in the box.)* Do I have to kill myself? Is this the end of my life?

EMILY: No, Victoria. This is the beginning of your life.

ANNE: *(Caressing Victoria's wrist.)* You can get the feeling you had when you starved yourself. You can get that feeling again, without doing harm to your insides. Just cut here, and make sure not to enter the vein.

EMILY: You can get that feeling, and you can share it with us.

ANNE: We understand you.

EMILY: Because we've been there.

ANNE: We were in pain. Insufferable pain.

EMILY: And now we've been set free.

VICTORIA: I want to believe you. I want to feel free. When I look into your eyes, I see my reflection, I see the pain in my own eyes, and I see the look of relief in yours. I see that there is a way out from my suffering, and a better way to live. I see that there is a better life before me, and a closeness that I've never experienced before. *(Thrusting her hands toward Emily and Anne.)* Here. Here are my wrists.
(Blackout.)

END OF PLAY

Is Hope Dead?

JOE APPLEGATE

Is Hope Dead? was originally produced by The Parish
Players (P.O. Box 136, Thetford, Vt. 05074) on February 9,
10, and 11, 2007, at the Eclipse Grange Theatre in
Thetford, Vt. It was directed by Nora Jacobson and produced
by Dan Deneen; lighting design by Stephen Campbell;
the stage manager was Rebecca Young-Ward. The cast was as
follows: Don — David Keane, Nina — Susanne Dudley
Schon, Larry — Ethan Cole.

CHARACTERS

    DON: a copy editor, retirement age

    NINA: assistant managing editor, much younger than Don

    LARRY: a copy kid, younger than Nina

SETTING

    A newsroom on the East Coast, spacious, no cubicles, just desks, computers, phones, and a television set

TIME

    Around midnight on April 16, 2003

• • •

At rise: Don at his desk, finishing up some work. He checks his watch, puts away a pencil, stretches, yawns . . . turns off his computer. He is signing off for the night. Larry hurries past, tossing newspapers on the desks.

DON: Thanks, Larry.

LARRY: Hi, Don. Did Nina get ahold of you?

DON: No.

LARRY: Hope's dead. You sticking around?

DON: *(Gets up, puts on his overcoat.)* Nah, I'm taking the buyout.

LARRY: I meant about Hope being dead.

DON: That's what I'm saying, I have no choice. I say no, they fire me, I get nothing after twenty-two years.

    (Larry tries to move on.)

    How's your dad?

LARRY: OK.

DON: The last guy in America with a pension. I told him that pension of his is off of my back. Did he tell you that?

LARRY: *(Trying to leave.)* He told me.

DON: I went along with the strike, did what I thought was right. I come back, see where they put me? Back here with the copy kids. I used to be up front. I had fifteen years working days, and now here I am going home at midnight. I come back, the freelancers and part-timers are ahead of me, and now they want to throw me out. Well, that's OK, you know? They can have this crappy job . . . *(Seeing Larry's reaction.)* Yeah, sure.

And you know what they'll do when I'm gone? They'll get two or three part-timers in here.

LARRY: Don, I gotta run these papers around.

DON: I asked you a question. You're a part-timer.

LARRY: Yeah.

DON: No benefits.

LARRY: Not yet.

DON: No. You gotta work a thousand hours. Question: Did you get scheduled for a thousand hours last year?

LARRY: No.

DON: So you got screwed.

LARRY: I took some time off.

DON: You took some time off.

LARRY: To write.

DON: To write.

LARRY: And take care of my son.

DON: *(Beat.)* Oh. Congratulations.

   (Larry tries to leave again.)

   But, you know, just for the record, we used to do things in a way where one person made enough money to take care of two people at home. See what I'm saying? You work part-time and say your wife works full-time, or you work full-time and your wife works part-time, and who's the ultimate beneficiary of that? Not you, not your wife, not your son. It's this guy *(Points upstairs.)* And the shareholders, of course.

LARRY: Right. I gotta go.

DON: OK, get out of here. *(Prevents him from leaving again.)* Of course, Nina, she goes part-time for five years and comes back as my supervisor. She's the big star, the daughter of all the Seven Sisters, lacrosse captain, and she doesn't even know grammar. She wants it "friend of John's," you know, with the apostrophe, when it's supposed to be—

LARRY: Whoa, here she comes now. Maybe you better sign back on.

DON: What's up?

LARRY: I told you, Bob Hope is dead.

DON: What? You didn't say that.

LARRY: Yeah, I did, just now.

   (Don sits down at the desk.)

DON: Oh, God, oh no, oh Jesus. When did you hear?

LARRY: About an hour ago. It's on the Web. I wondered why you were going home.

DON: Jesus Christ! Fuck! I'm going to get fired. I am going to get nothing.

NINA: *(Entering.)* Larry, nobody's picking up downstairs. Go tell Eddie to hold the home edition, none of the papers leave the building. Go.

LARRY: I don't know if we can do that, tonight, Nina, you see —

NINA: Go!

LARRY: I'll tell Eddie.

(Larry exits.)

NINA: *(To Don.)* CNN has Bob Hope dead, what's on the wire?

DON: Ah . . .

NINA: Am I seeing this? You're not signed on.

DON: Signing on now.

NINA: *(Noticing his coat.)* Look at you. You're going home.

DON: Give me a second.

NINA: Don, it's not even eleven-thirty!

DON: I'm sorry.

NINA: Sorry!

DON: The wire was quiet.

NINA: We're going to have to throw out the first run, Don, that's seven thousand papers, that's *money*. I have to sign reports.

DON: Yes, I'm sorry, OK? Am I the only one in the building?

NINA: *(Picks up newspaper on Don's desk, looks at front page and jump page.)* You're the one who's supposed to be watching the wire. You have really screwed up here.

DON: Nina, I am sorry. I am. I did screw up. I apologize.

NINA: I have had it with you. I am *done. (Dials phone on Don's desk.)* Eddie? Nina. Did Don talk to you? . . . Didn't think so . . . OK — we're re-plating A-one and A-fourteen for the home edition, and — what? No, no, no . . . this has to happen, Eddie . . . We *do* have time, we have to get this on page one. We can have it to you in, what? *(To Don.)* ten minutes?

DON: Five.

NINA: *(Into phone.)* Five minutes. OK.

(Hangs up. To Don.)

They have to stuff inserts tonight. We have got to get this done fast.

DON: "We." I like that.

NINA: Well — OK, then, can you really do this?

DON: There should be an obit ready to go in the media basket. We'll swap out the lead package and trim the jump. I can do this. OK, I'm signed on.

NINA: Check the wire.

DON: I am. *(Beat.)* This is very strange. What is going on?

NINA: What?

DON: There's no wire story.

NINA: Of course there is.

DON: No, there's just a news alert advisory: CNN Web site reports Bob Hope has died at home in Toluca Lake.

NINA: Go to the site.

DON: OK. *(Beat.)* There's nothing on their front page.

NINA: Click there.

DON: OK, there's the obit. But why isn't it on the front page of the site?

NINA: Call A.P.

DON: *(Dialing.)* Like they would know. When was it, ten years ago, they put his obit on the wire by mistake? There was a senator eulogizing him on the floor of Congress, and a day later Hope is going, "I'm not dead. I'm just so old they canceled my blood type."
(Into phone.) National desk, hurry. Yeah, Don Howard at transmission code N-Y-one-zero-zero-nine. OK, we're trying to check if Bob Hope died. The comedian. We need to confirm that right now. OK, call me back, fast. No, no, I am asking you please to call me back, at . . . will you take my phone number? I want to give you my number. I'm just asking for some service here. We're supposed to be working for each other, you fucking fuck, and you won't call me back? What's your name?

NINA: Don, let me talk.

DON: I asked for your name!

NINA: Don, just . . .

DON: Fucking punk ass kid hung up.

NINA: What did he say?

DON: I am so sick of rude young people.

NINA: Tell me!

DON: He said he couldn't call back because he expected to get a lot more calls, so we're supposed to wait for the story.

NINA: We have to go with our story. Get the pages ready to go.

DON: But what's the story? We have one Web page that says he's dead. That's it.

NINA: If there's no story then we hold the changes, but we need to be ready.

DON: OK. You're the boss.

NINA: Yeah, Don — I am the boss, and you know what that means, really? That means I don't have the guild to protect me when I screw up. To-morrow morning, if Hope is dead on TV, and he's not dead in the paper, what am I going to —

DON: I am trying to work here! OK? Go back to your office.

NINA: If you had been doing your job half an hour ago we'd be OK. Why can't you focus?

DON: Focus. Preppy lacrosse bullshit. What are you, my life coach? I have pulled more long hours, you have no idea, none whatsoever. We used to put out four editions, we worked like horses, pulling this piece of shit wagon, and you come along, a part-timer filing bullshit society stories from home in your pajamas —

NINA: We're in trouble here because you were asleep. That's what we're dealing with right now.

DON: You want me to do this? Huh? Or you want me to walk out? I don't need this abuse.

NINA: Doing your job is abuse.

DON: Can you lay these pages out in Quark? Can you?

NINA: No, I can't.

DON: Can you write a headline?

NINA: No.

DON: I got a headline for you. *(Typing.)* "Hope Is Probably Dead"? And it fits!

NINA: Take that off the page!

DON: I am so sick of your yuppie bullshit. Your bullshit part-time job. How do you work part-time for five years and come back as my boss?

NINA: Oh here we go, it all comes out. Raging bull! Thirty thousand years of privilege and the minute somebody different gets a break —

DON: Every change around here benefits you, personally, but I'm the one standing on my head at midnight doing the work. —

NINA: Benefits? *Benefits? You pay nothing for health care, you get seven weeks off, you never work a holiday.* I came back full-time just for the health insurance. You pay nothing. You know. And here's the thing — your union sensibilities. Did you even ask, once, how much gets taken out of my check for health insurance? In addition to all the other dues I have paid?

DON: Dues.

NINA: Yes! You have no idea. You roll around here, the radical union guy, the great sage and pious liberal, but you don't actually do your job —

DON: OK, that's it! I have edited your copy! I have saved your ass so many times!

(Larry enters.)

LARRY: Hey guys . . .

NINA: You! have a bad attitude, you're lazy, you're a grouch, you're a pompous old fart . . . and . . . and . . . and one more thing. It's "friend of John's" not "friend of John."

LARRY: Guys?

DON: No, no, no, no. You were wrong five years ago, you are wrong now. "Friend of John's" is double negative, I mean possessive.

LARRY: Hey! Hell-o?

NINA: Do people say "friend of me"? You are out of your mind!

DON: Double possessive genitive is the technical term.

NINA: People say "friend of mine." Is that double possessive genitive?

DON: Of course not!

NINA: Of course it is!

DON: "Mine" is the possessive case. The "of" is a simple preposition.

(Don and Nina speak over each other.)

You know Fowler? You ever heard of Fowler?

NINA: We write it how people say it . . . and yes, I've heard of Fowler. In the *latest* edition —

DON: *(Stands.)* You think I'm ungrammatical, you think I am ungrammatical! I will not take that from you! You finish the page! Go ahead.

NINA: This can't be happening.

DON: I said you finish the page.

(Don starts to leave.)

NINA: I can't. You know that. Jesus, Don! Just do your job!

DON: I don't have a job! I want my job back! OK? I don't want to take the buyout. I want to keep working, at least for a couple of years. I'll die if I have to quit. I don't know how to do anything else.

LARRY: 'Scuse me?

NINA: Larry, it's coming.

LARRY: But—

NINA: Larry . . .

(Larry sits down and watches TV.)

DON: I need help, Nina. I need somebody to say a word. I screwed this up, I admit that. I owe you big time. Can you help me out?

Because, you know, I am pretty good at certain things.

(Sits back down at his desk and starts working.)

There they are, two new pages, ready to go. Twenty-two years, Nina.

NINA: OK.

DON: I apologize again. How about it?

NINA: I want someone on my side, too, Don.

DON: I can do that, I think.

NINA: Call Eddie.

LARRY: *(Looking up from TV.)* You don't need to. We don't need the changes. Hope's not dead.

NINA: *(To Larry.)* You're joking.

LARRY: Nope. He's alive. It was on the CNN site. I came up tell you, but you were having a grammar fight.

NINA: What did it say?

LARRY: Somebody's password expired and a bunch of dummy obit pages got turned on by default.

DON: You sure?

LARRY: It's all over the site. I was watching it till I came up.

NINA: Good thinking.

LARRY: Eddie told me to.

NINA: So, I guess he can start the press run.

LARRY: He did.

NINA: Good. Well! That's good news. Don, you stick around for a while, see if the A.P. moves anything on the mistake. If they do before the last press run, brief it on the back page. OK?

DON: No problem.

NINA: Well — good night, you guys.

(Stops before leaving.) And you proofed the A-section, right Don?

DON: Yes, Nina, about an hour ago.

NINA: Good night.

(Nina exits.)

DON: *(Sotto voce, to Larry.)* I was right all along!

LARRY: Oh yeah, Don. You're sick right. I'll see ya.

(Larry exits.)

DON: Say hi to your dad. Tell him I'm still here, *(To himself.)* and I still got a job, thank God. Bob Hope is, what? A hundred years old. I always liked him. He's pretty funny.

(Curtain.)

END OF PLAY

The Man Who Shot Santa Claus

CARL L. WILLIAMS

Produced by Phare Play Productions, Producers Club,
New York City, November 17–19, 2006, as part of
"Inside Carl's Shorts," an evening of one-acts. Directed by
Roland Uruci with the following cast: Prosecutor —
Jen Brooks, Defense — Niae Knight, O'Banion — Susan
Tietze. (Note: The director chose to cast a woman as O'Banion
and call it "The Woman Who Shot Santa Claus,"
but O'Banion is intended to be a man.) Also produced in
Scriptwriters/Houston Ten by Ten; Crosscurrents Five & Dime
Festival (Kansas City.); Barestage Theatre Six 10's @ Eight
Festival (Red Bluff, Calif.).

CHARACTERS
 PROSECUTOR: tough and idealistic, female
 DEFENSE: crafty lawyer, male
 O'BANION: defendant, sourpuss

SETTING
 Courtroom, one witness chair, two opposing counsel tables

TIME
 Present

• • •

At rise: O'Banion sits in the witness chair, being interrogated by Prosecutor. Defense sits taking notes.

PROSECUTOR: Mr. O'Banion, you sit in court today, in the presence of this jury . . . *(Indicates audience.)* . . . accused of a heinous crime — a crime more despicable than any I've encountered in my years as a prosecutor.

O'BANION: It's all a mistake.

PROSECUTOR: Is it not a fact that on the night of December 24th — Christmas Eve — you did shoot and kill the personage known as Santa Claus? *(Pulls a red Santa hat from a bag on the table.)*

O'BANION: Yes, but I didn't mean to. I thought he was a prowler.

PROSECUTOR: A prowler. A three-hundred-pound prowler in a red suit with a huge bag full of toys?

O'BANION: It was dark.

PROSECUTOR: Was it? Isn't it true, Mr. O'Banion — and I have witnesses I could call — that your practice was to leave your Christmas tree lights burning all night?

O'BANION: Well, yes, I usually —

PROSECUTOR: So on the night in question, weren't those lights burning?

O'BANION: I guess maybe they were.

PROSECUTOR: And the body was found where, Mr. O'Banion?

O'BANION: *(Reluctantly.)* By the tree.

PROSECUTOR: Please tell the jury how many times you shot him.

O'BANION: *(Mutters.)* Five times.

PROSECUTOR: Louder, so the court can hear.

O'BANION: Five. I shot him five times.

PROSECUTOR: You shot Santa Claus five times by the light of the Christmas tree. And you still maintain you mistook him for a prowler?

DEFENSE: Objection. My client already answered that question.

PROSECUTOR: Then I'll ask another. Mr. O'Banion, I have here a folder of affidavits taken from your relatives, friends, and co-workers, all of whom attest to your frequently stated animosity toward Santa Claus. Isn't it fair to say you hated Santa?

O'BANION: I wouldn't say I hated him.

PROSECUTOR: You didn't like him.

O'BANION: Not especially, no.

PROSECUTOR: Why was that?

O'BANION: Lots of reasons. He took credit for things he didn't do. How many gifts did I buy my kids every Christmas, and who did they thank? Santa.

PROSECUTOR: You're not claiming he never brought them anything?

O'BANION: Oh, sure. Some cheap little homemade toys and a sockful of hard candy.

PROSECUTOR: More than that.

O'BANION: Yeah, well, that's all I ever got.

PROSECUTOR: Really? When?

O'BANION: When I was a kid. I wrote Santa, just like everybody else. But on Christmas Day, when the other kids were out riding their new bikes and skating past me on the sidewalk, I was sitting there with a little wooden truck and a two-bit bag of sour balls.

PROSECUTOR: No need to ask if you'd been naughty or nice.

O'BANION: And yet he had the gall to laugh that laugh of his. Ho-ho-ho! All the time. Like he was rubbing it in. Here's a jawbreaker, kid. Ho-ho-ho! The sadist.

PROSECUTOR: So your resentment deepened through the years, until it grew into hatred. Isn't that right?

O'BANION: OK, sure. I hated him.

PROSECUTOR: Then Christmas Eve you waited for him to come, didn't you? Waited with a gun in your hand. Waited in the stillness.

O'BANION: Not a creature was stirring. Then whoosh — here he came, feet first down the chimney.

PROSECUTOR: Did he say anything when he saw you?

O'BANION: He just stood there laughing at me. That's when I shot him. Right between the ho's.

PROSECUTOR: And you did it on purpose — didn't you? Didn't you!

O'BANION: Yes, yes, I did it! And I'm glad I shot him! He had it coming. I've rid the earth of its annual scourge of greed, envy, and disappointment! They should build a monument to me in appreciation.

PROSECUTOR: A monument to murder. Self-confessed. The prosecution rests. *(O'Banion appears shaken as Prosecutor takes a seat and Defense rises.)*

DEFENSE: Well, now. Madam Prosecutor has managed to muddy the waters, hasn't she? I would like to remind the jury that just because my client shot and killed Santa Claus, that doesn't make him guilty of murder. *(Slips the Santa hat back in the bag.)*

O'BANION: That's right.

DEFENSE: First of all, it has yet to be established that Santa Claus was even human. If he wasn't human, there could be no murder.

PROSECUTOR: The victim was shot dead.

DEFENSE: Physical demise is not exclusive to human beings. But passing over that for now, let's examine the character of this Santa Claus, aka Kris Kringle, aka St. Nicholas, aka . . . well, who knows how many other aliases he operated under? Mr. O'Banion, did you invite Santa Claus to your home on the night of December 24th?

O'BANION: I certainly did not.

DEFENSE: Would you say, then, he was an intruder?

O'BANION: Definitely.

DEFENSE: Had he ever broken into your house before?

O'BANION: Repeatedly, ever since my children were born.

DEFENSE: What is the age of your oldest child?

O'BANION: Sixteen. The youngest is five.

DEFENSE: Let me understand. For sixteen years now, this Santa Claus has been violating the sanctity of your home, creeping into your house, attracted in some perverse way by the presence of your children?

O'BANION: Yes, exactly.

DEFENSE: That must have been frightening.

O'BANION: It was. Frightening.

DEFENSE: Did you feel threatened?

O'BANION: I felt threatened.

DEFENSE: Did he take anything during these break-ins?

O'BANION: He sure did. Cookies . . . milk . . . pieces of fruit.

DEFENSE: Was he destructive in any way?

O'BANION: I'll say he was! You should get on top of my house and look at the shingle damage from his sleigh. Not to mention what those nine reindeer left on my roof.

DEFENSE: Ah, yes . . . the reindeer. Were you aware the SPCA was investigating their maltreatment at the hands of the deceased?

PROSECUTOR: Objection! Relevance? I could just as well talk about those poor elves who lost their home and livelihood when your client blew away their employer.

DEFENSE: "Poor elves" is right. Toiling away in that sweatshop run by Commandant Claus, who should've been charged with elf abuse.

PROSECUTOR: They were cast out in the snow when Santa died.

DEFENSE: Totally false. They relocated to China and went to work for Reebok.

O'BANION: *(Tentative.)* Excuse me.

PROSECUTOR: What do you want?

O'BANION: Have you noticed the judge isn't saying anything?

DEFENSE: The judge fell asleep twenty minutes ago.

O'BANION: Shouldn't we wake him up?

PROSECUTOR: And be charged with contempt?

DEFENSE: When he wakes up, he'll think he presided over the whole trial.

PROSECUTOR: Let's get on with it.

DEFENSE: Fine with me. Mr. O'Banion, wouldn't you say those long years of persecution by Mr. Claus, coupled with your very natural state of anxiety in the defense of your family, compelled you to grab a gun and shoot that predatory home invader?

O'BANION: Yes, I would say that.

DEFENSE: The defense rests. *(Pause, to Prosecutor.)* You may proceed with your summation.

PROSECUTOR: Thank you. *(O'Banion starts to get up.)* You stay where you are, where everyone can see you. *(Motions O'Banion back into the chair.)* Ladies and gentlemen of the jury, this man did willfully and with premeditation shoot and kill Santa Claus, a beloved figure who had done him no harm. With malice in his heart and a loaded revolver in his hand, he gunned down a defenseless, jolly old man who had brought joy to countless millions of children. What more needs to be said? I ask you to return a verdict of guilty as charged — of murder in the first degree. *(Prosecutor sits. Defense rises and addresses the jury.)*

DEFENSE: Yes, my client shot Santa Claus. He doesn't deny it. But just remember who — or what — it was he shot. A chronic housebreaker, a criminal trespasser, a vandal, a night-prowling weirdo in a red suit, a stalker of children, an elf-enslaving, reindeer-flogging stealer of cookies who left behind little wooden trucks and sour balls, all the while taking false credit for bicycles and baby dolls and every red wagon ever found beneath a Christmas tree. How many of you, I ask, once wrote to Santa for something your heart was set on? And how did it make you feel when you didn't get it? Do you remember how heartbroken you were? How devastated? How betrayed? No more will that charlatan hold out false promises to unsuspecting children the world over. When Mr. O'Banion pulled that trigger, he set the children free! I implore you to set Mr. O'Banion free, as well. Thank you.

(Defense returns to his table. A pause as they all look at each other uncertainly.)

O'BANION: Are we finished? Can I leave?

PROSECUTOR: No. You haven't been excused.

DEFENSE: What do we do now?

PROSECUTOR: I suppose we'll have to rouse the judge after all.

DEFENSE: To make the charge to the jury, etcetera, etcetera, blah blah blah.

(An Audience Member in the front row holds up a folded piece of paper.)

PROSECUTOR: Wait a minute. What is this?

DEFENSE: Don't tell me you've come to a decision already?

PROSECUTOR: *(Takes the paper.)* Is this your verdict?

DEFENSE: What does it say?

PROSECUTOR: *(Unfolds the paper, reads.)* Justifiable homicide.

O'BANION: Yes! Not guilty! And Santa's gone for good! *(Jumps out of the chair.)*

DEFENSE: *(Shakes his hand.)* Congratulations!

PROSECUTOR: *(Stares at the verdict.)* I refuse to accept this.

O'BANION: I owe everything to you.

DEFENSE: And I'll collect every bit of it.

O'BANION: Believe me, it was worth it.

PROSECUTOR: Mr. O'Banion . . . you may think you got away with murder, but you didn't really.

O'BANION: Santa's dead, isn't he?

PROSECUTOR: *(With great emotion.)* No, Santa Claus isn't dead. He never will be. As long as there's a child with a dream . . . as long as a tiny heart beats faster with hope . . . as long as little feet run with anticipation to meet a bright tomorrow, Santa Claus will live!

O'BANION: *(Pause, then to Defense.)* Can I shoot her, too?

(Blackout.)

END OF PLAY

One Night at Your Local Superstore

JENNY LYN BADER

One Night at Your Local Superstore was commissioned by
WORKS Productions and was first performed in their Reader's
Theatre series of world premiere plays by Jenny Lyn Bader, *The
Superstore Cycle,* at Barnes & Noble, Lincoln Center in New
York City, produced by Julian Rad and directed by Hilary
Adams, with the following cast: Greg — James Hay, Milton —
Michael Shawn Montgomery, Carol Ann — Danielle Skraastad.
The play's premiere production was at Café Theatre (David J.
Hoffman, Artistic Director.) at George St. Playhouse, in New
Brunswick, N.J., directed by Andrea Arden, with Joe Fellman as
Greg, Kristofer Updike as Milton, and Katya Campbell as
Carol Ann. Julie Kramer directed the 2006 production at
NYU/Strasberg with Reese Efler as Greg, Ryan Neller as Mil-
ton, and Karen Bjornst as Carol Ann. The play was remounted
by Café Theatre, directed by Rob Bradshaw, in 2007 at
Tierney's in Montclair, N.J., with Chet Herman as Greg,
Ben Clawson as Milton, and Jenelle Sosa as Carol Ann.

CHARACTERS

GREG: thirties to forties, an established man of letters
MILTON: twenties to thirties, a less-established literary type
CAROL ANN: twenties to thirties, a voracious reader

SETTING

The author's table at a bookstore

TIME

One night

PRODUCTION NOTES

The play can be performed with three actors. If more actors are available in the production, they can form a line waiting to get their books signed when the actors playing the authors are signing books. If not, the "line" can be implied.

•   •   •

Your local superstore. Behind the author's table, Milton is signing books. As he signs, he appears anxious, clearly worried about something. Greg, a good-looking, self-loving man, waits on the book-signing line. A young woman, Carol Ann, stands on line behind Greg. As Milton finishes signing a book, Greg interrupts:

GREG: Milton!

MILTON: *(Startled.)* Hm? Oh yes. Ah — Greg! Hi.

GREG: *(Pretending to be congratulatory.)* That was some presentation! It was . . . not bad. Not bad at all.

MILTON: Your pep talk beforehand was helpful.

GREG: In my own presentations I tend to try for more — polish. But what I liked about yours was the very lack of polish. The rough edges.

MILTON: Thank you.

GREG: So I wanted to congratulate you.

MILTON: That's very generous, considering you're just about to — don't you need . . . ?

GREG: Not at all. I always like to watch one before mine. Puts me in the right mood.

MILTON: I'm signing as fast as I can, so I can send the audience over.

GREG: Oh, don't worry about that. I'm sure we don't have the same readers. I write about what drives the human soul, you write about building . . . buildings.

MILTON: Did you bring a book?

GREG: Oh no, I didn't want to put you in the awkward position of feeling obligated to buy my book after I bought yours.

MILTON: That's very considerate. Thanks.

GREG: You're welcome. Good luck.

(Greg exits. Carol Ann now has the first place in line. She is exuberant, hypnotic.)

CAROL ANN: Hi.

MILTON: Hi.

CAROL ANN: Wow.

(She sets down her book and stares at Milton.)

Wow!

(As Carol Ann stares at him intently, Milton becomes even more nervous than he was before.)

MILTON: To whom should I make it out?

CAROL ANN: Carol. *(Beat.)* Ann.

MILTON: Which one? Carol or Ann?

CAROL ANN: No. It's one name. *(Dictating.)* "To Carol Ann Vilna Fitzpatrick Norman."

MILTON: Is that it?

CAROL ANN: Comma.

MILTON: Comma.

CAROL ANN: "Who has dedicated herself to the serious reading of my work like no one else, who cares deeply about my theory of the relatively new in pre-postmodern architecture . . . And who is a very good listener."

MILTON: *(Scribbling quickly to keep up with her.)* Really.

CAROL ANN: Mm hmm!

MILTON: *(Finishes writing and stares at her, then apologizes.)* I should probably, um — sign the next person's book.

CAROL ANN: There's no next person. I'm last.

MILTON: *(Looking over.)* Were there not just a few more — people?

CAROL ANN: The ones on line behind me? They just went to Greg Carlson's reading.

(She whispers, conspiratorial.)

There are people who go to every reading at this store. Indiscriminately.

MILTON: I didn't realize.

CAROL ANN: It is such an exceptional pleasure to meet you.

MILTON: But we haven't really —

CAROL ANN: Ever since your first 500-word piece that hinted towards it in *Architectural Currents Quarterly*, I have looked forward to this book.

MILTON: *(Surprised.)* You read the 500-word piece in *Architectural Currents Quarterly?*

(Beat. She nods.)

I should probably get going . . .

CAROL ANN: Why, are you married?

MILTON: No! Not married. No. That wasn't what I —

CAROL ANN: Then why don't you let me buy you a cappuccino?

MILTON: *(Quickly.)* OK.

CAROL ANN: Here.

(She hands Milton a cappuccino.)

MILTON: Uh. I'm not married. But I should tell you . . .

CAROL ANN: The part in your book I love most is the chapter on the revival of passion.

MILTON: *(He stares at her. For too long. He breaks it off.)* Sorry. I . . .

CAROL ANN: Do you have a favorite footnote?

MILTON: In history?

CAROL ANN: In your book.

MILTON: *(Brightens up.)* That would have to be footnote 37.

CAROL ANN: Mm that's a good one. Definitely top five. That's where you make fun of both —

MILTON & CAROL ANN: *(Laughing.)* Frank Lloyd Wright and Foucault!

CAROL ANN: That's remarkable, that you knew that. Most writers have a research assistant number the footnotes.

MILTON: It's more remarkable that you knew it. Most readers do not recall footnote numbers.

CAROL ANN: I have a pretty good memory. Gets me into trouble sometimes.

MILTON: How could having a good memory get you into trouble?

CAROL ANN: The way I remember what I see or read upsets those around me. I retain . . . odd things.

MILTON: Like what?

CAROL ANN: Like I once met a guy at a party, recognized his name, from a magazine, so I said, hey didn't you used to be assistant science editor of *Playboy?* And he was! But he was a bit . . . startled. It's numbers, it's names. — Film credits stay with me. I'll remember the gaffer. The best boy. The grip.

MILTON: Oh, I always like to see who the grip is!

CAROL ANN: Sure, you look. But you don't allow it to stay with you.

MILTON: So your memory is photographic.

CAROL ANN: No. Just compulsive.

MILTON: That's great! I wish I had a better memory. I forget things all the time.

CAROL ANN: Like what?

MILTON: I don't know . . . um. Like the other day I was trying to remember the height of the statue of Athena in the Acropolis when I know it's —

CAROL ANN: Forty-two feet.

MILTON: Yes, exactly! Forty-two feet. Sometimes I do worse. I'll go to the library and forget what book I wanted. Or I'll dial a number and forget who I just called.

CAROL ANN: Oh sure, I've done that. I'm not —

MILTON: I most often forget what I was about to say.

CAROL ANN: What *were* you about to say?

MILTON: What?

CAROL ANN: Before. You said you had something to tell me.

MILTON: I don't know . . . *(He remembers and is alarmed.)* Oh God! I know! If I told you, then you would hate me. So it's just as well I didn't. Thanks for the cappuccino —

CAROL ANN: I could never hate you, Milton Framingham. You rock my world. Yours is the only superstore reading I have ever cared about. Your aesthetic atavism is my inspiration.

MILTON: But I —

CAROL ANN: There is nothing you could tell me that would make me hate you. In fact, the more I talk to you . . .
(She kisses him.)

CAROL ANN: *(Continued.)* I'm sorry. This must happen to you all the time. Women throwing themselves at you at book signings . . .

MILTON: No actually I haven't done much of this sort of thing —

CAROL ANN: Women don't throw themselves at you?

MILTON: I mean, I haven't done many book signings.

CAROL ANN: Of course you have. You've been on an entire book tour in
(Reels them off quickly and easily.)
Chicago, Detroit, Minneapolis, Dallas, San Francisco, Los Angeles, Austin, Atlanta, Washington, Baltimore —

MILTON: Wow. You know the whole . . .

CAROL ANN: *(Upset with herself.)* Sorry. There I go again with the memory . . . I always ruin everything with the memory!

MILTON: No I'm the one who —

CAROL ANN: I don't want to ruin it. Because meeting you in person is even better than I imagined. You're warmer and more accessible than your literary persona. You're equally insightful but wiser and more grounded.

MILTON: *(Thrilled.)* You think so?

CAROL ANN: Yes.

MILTON: Good in that case I will tell you.

(He looks around carefully to make sure no one is listening, then reveals.)

I'm not Milton Framingham.

CAROL ANN: What?

OK SO HE'S NOT REALLY MILTON: Please, please don't tell anyone.

CAROL ANN: Of course not. What a horrible — Where the hell is he?

NO HE'S NOT MILTON: Milton's home in bed. He's got a 104 fever and a limp.

CAROL ANN: A limp??

HE'S JUST "MILTON": The book tour just about killed Milton. He sprained his ankle running down the tarmac in the Dallas airport. He wasn't in good shape to begin with. And now the flu. He wanted to cancel tonight, but there was so much advertising, they even announced it on his favorite radio station, W-H-O-A . . .

CAROL ANN: I heard.

"MILTON": — and this was his first superstore reading. It meant a lot to him, to read here.

CAROL ANN: But he didn't —

"MILTON": Or at least to have someone who looked like him read here.

CAROL ANN: You *do* look like him!

"MILTON": I know. It's uncanny isn't it?

CAROL ANN: But how do you know about footnote 37?

"MILTON": I'm his research assistant.

CAROL ANN: *(Disgusted.)* Oh God.

"MILTON": Ever since I started working for him, people said I looked like him, and we made these jokes about how one day I should do one of his appearances . . . Ha, ha, we had to go try it.

CAROL ANN: Ha.

"MILTON": Look —

CAROL ANN: You signed his name! This is . . . a forgery!

"MILTON": No, it's pretty genuine. I do have to sign his name frequently to get into certain libraries. I've practiced it a lot. At this point I sign his name more like him than he does.

CAROL ANN: Right.

"MILTON": *(Pleading, with great conviction.)* Listen, Carol Ann Vilna Fitzpatrick Norman. Neither of us has ever done anything like this before. We lead upstanding lives. We do research. This is beyond our wildest — We never thought one of us would pretend to be the other one reading in a superstore. We just work hard and, for the most part, thanklessly. Milton's publisher would kill him if someone didn't show up tonight in the capacity of Milton. Of course we considered the literary implications, the legal implications, but I never considered . . .

CAROL ANN: What?

"MILTON": I just . . . never thought that I'd meet someone so lovely while impersonating Milton.

(Beat. It looks like she might buy it.)

I certainly never thought I'd meet someone who appreciates my work on footnote 37. So I thought I should tell you. Before kissing any further.

(She considers this idea as if tempted.)

CAROL ANN: Mm hmm it's too bad you're not him . . . you're a great kisser.

"MILTON": Thanks.

CAROL ANN: So you *do* work for Milton Framingham.

"MILTON": Yes.

CAROL ANN: So you could, for example, introduce me to Milton.

"MILTON": If that's what you wanted.

CAROL ANN: Right.

"MILTON": *(Miserable.)* Is that what you want?

(She stares at him as if he is lovely.)

CAROL ANN: Oh lord.

"MILTON":What?

CAROL ANN: Before I came here, I thought I wanted to meet Milton. Then I thought I wanted to meet you. But now . . . *(Beat.)* I don't think I should get mixed up with either of you.

"MILTON": I understand. And I hope — you're not too disillusioned. Despite this little prank Milton is really a good person. And at bottom, so am I. By the way, I'm —

CAROL ANN: You're Nathaniel Bell.

ACTUALLY HIS NAME IS NATHANIEL: Yes. How did you —

CAROL ANN: *(Miserable.)* I remember you. You're in the acknowledgments.

NATHANIEL: I'm also in the phone book, if you ever.

CAROL ANN: Thanks. If I ever get over this, I'll think about calling you. Nat.

NAT: I am so sorry. It was great meeting you. Good luck, um, forgetting about this, if that's what you want. Or call me. Good night. *(Nat exits, miserable.)*

(Carol watches him go. She looks sad. Then she waits till she's sure he's gone. Perks up. Starts laughing. Then from her superstore shopping bag she pulls out another book . . . and a fresh cappuccino. She cuts the line for Greg Carlson's reading.)

CAROL ANN: Excuse me Mr. Carlson — would you sign my book?

GREG: I'm sorry, I didn't see you there. How should I make it out?

CAROL ANN: To Carol . . . Ann . . . Vilna Fitzpatrick Norman. *(Beat.)* Comma.

END OF PLAY

Past Lives

Jenny Lyn Bader

Past Lives premiered at Henlopen Theatre Project in Delaware, directed by Ari Laura Kreith. The cast was: Nell — Gwendolyn Walker, Bill — Connor Barrett, Janet — Alysia Reiner. An earlier, thirty-minute incarnation of this play premiered at Center Stage N.Y., where it was directed by Dan Fields in the evening of plays *Emotionally Correct*, with Jennie Israel as Nell, David Alan Basche as Bill, and Lisa Heilbrunn as Janet. Julie Kramer directed that version when *Emotionally Correct* was remounted at Center Stage N.Y. with Victoria Soyer as Nell, Jeff O'Malley as Bill, and Lisa Heilbrunn as Janet. Ms. Kramer also directed the most recent incarnation of *Past Lives* with Jessica Foreman as Nell, Mardee Bennett as Bill, and Kathryn Maykish as Janet, at NYU's Lee Strasberg Institute.

CHARACTERS
   BILL: thirties to forties, a psychotherapist
   JANET: thirties to forties, a past lives–regression therapist
   NELL: twenties, a waitress

SETTING
   A macrobiotic coffee shop

TIME
   Lunchtime

.   .   .

Nell is setting café tables and adding dispensers of chutney and organic sea salt. Bill runs in, panting.

BILL: Can I have this table?
NELL: Sure, if you order. *(She stares at Bill penetratingly and smiles. He smiles back.)* You've got something in your hair. Is that soap?
   (She exits. Bill examines himself in a spoon. Janet floats in; she is attractive, effusive, and clad in flowy skirts. She hugs Bill.)
JANET: Bill! You are a friend! You've got something in your hair. Is that soap?
   (He runs his hands through his hair, trying to remove the soap.)
BILL: I . . . was in the shower when you called . . . Uh — What did he do this time?
JANET: Maybe I just need to talk it through . . . *(Launches in.)* Yesterday, I had a meeting. With the *mayor's wife*. She wanted her lives done. Had to be top-secret, since ever since Nancy Reagan had that meeting with my friend Joan —
BILL: Joan?
JANET: Joan Quigley. The psychic.
BILL: You know Nancy Reagan's astrologer? *(Catches himself quickly, careful not to offend Janet.)* I mean, psychic.
JANET: We did healing training together. Laying on of hands. All right, I get to Gracie Mansion, and the mayor wants his lives done too.
BILL: You're kidding. I wouldn't have thought . . .
JANET: I know! So I'm channeling the mayor and his wife — most important job I've done besides the Dalai Lama's cousin — and their past lives are remarkable.

BILL: As remarkable as their current lives?

JANET: The mayor made a lot of the same mistakes he's making now? During the Roman Empire. The wife hasn't had career satisfaction since the twelfth century, when she was a court poet, and even then she had to sleep around . . . So I'm trying to give this all some positive spin, when Greg pages me. — And for once I don't call him back right away, because I'm . . . reincarnating City Hall here!

BILL: Of course you are!

JANET: But he keeps beeping so I call and the security guy is standing right there and I can't tell Greg where I am. So I say I'm busy . . . *(Realizing.)* which is the quality he seems to find most alluring . . . and he yells at me. I yell back, the guard thinks I'm behaving aggressively, he demands that I be strip-searched.

BILL: Oh Janet.

JANET: So they find the charm chain my guru gave me when he died and they get all huffy because it looks metal but it didn't set off the metal detector so what the hell is it. I tell them it's a *transcendent object,* of course it wouldn't set off a metal detector!

(Bill nods.)

That's when they decide to test it for plutonium. Now the mayor's upset, understandably he wants the reading finished before he approves the city budget. I try to help but I'm distracted . . . *(Miserable.)* I think I messed up the budget for the whole fiscal year! But instead of comforting me when I get home, Greg is jealous *he* didn't do a reading for the mayor. And he says he can't speak to me while he works through his jealousy.

BILL: Janet you can't let him treat you like this! If you just thought . . . more highly of yourself, maybe? . . . Had better self-esteem? Then you wouldn't let him manipulate you.

JANET: *(Upset with herself.)* What do you mean? How could I have low self-esteem? I run self-esteem workshops. I do regression consultations for royalty and politicians. I did the House minority whip! I did Princess Anne. I write articles on self-esteem for very popular newsletters. How could I possibly fall prey to that?

BILL: I don't know. You're right.

JANET: You're not supposed to tell me I have low self-esteem. You're supposed to tell me everything will work out, this is just a phase.

BILL: Everything will work out.

JANET: *(Delighted.)* You really think so?

BILL: This is just a phase. *(Beat.)* But phases can last . . . centuries, Janet.

JANET: You're telling me?

(The U-2 song "With or Without You" starts playing.)

I can't believe they're playing this song. This place has the funniest karma.

BILL: Well, I don't know about karma, but this is the place that you and I — first had lunch. Um, together. You know. I cherish . . . our lunches, Janet.

JANET: Me too. You're so supportive.

BILL: That's what you need Janet. Supportiveness. More than you need . . . er, Greg . . .

JANET: But Greg can be surprisingly supportive.

BILL: When?

JANET: During our past lives. I found out, when we went into trance this weekend, that in the sixteenth century he was really there for me!

BILL: He was?

JANET: At the retreat, we got hypnotized by our mentor, Zürki? In the lifetime I remembered, in the 1500s, we had a deep bond. He was my brother. Greg saw I was a gentle soul and defended me from our cruel father. Then, to escape the household, I married. We never saw each other again!

BILL: *(Not sure what to say.)* Gosh.

JANET: *(Knowingly.)* Mmm *hmm!* And in the 1800s he adored me. Greg remembered this one . . .

(Nell enters.)

Nineteenth century. I was a prominent minister.

(Nell stands by their table in time to hear their next exchange.)

BILL: *You* were a prominent minister?

JANET: In England. The Anglican Church, they had women ministers.

NELL: Are you ready to order?

JANET: Yes I'd like the organic wild tuna on pita with bean sprouts no tomato with a side of avocado and a soy chai latte he wants the vegetarian lasagna right Bill you were going to order that weren't you and can you bring us some ice water now just lightly iced but no ice in mine?

(Nell nods and exits.)

He was a young woman in my congregation who fell in love with me. It was scandalous. We were lesbians in the nineteenth century! Can you imagine how hard it was for us? Later, I got married, had kids. But he never recovered from it. Spent the rest of that life not recovering from it. Suffering because of *his* love for *me.*

BILL: And now . . . ?

JANET: I don't know. On one hand, we need to break the cycle — you know, get together in *this* life.

(Bill nods. Janet continues.)

On the other hand, I mean . . .

(She pauses, then, exasperated, blurts out.)

He's *married!*

(An awkward pause as they sit alone, and Bill tries to figure out what to say but then just re-arranges his napkin.)

BILL: Yeah, it's . . .

(Nell enters with the water.)

JANET: Excuse me, I said no ice in my ice water.

NELL: Right. Sorry. No ice in your ice water.

(She pours ice back into a pitcher as she listens.)

BILL: *(Concerned.)* Does he . . . have kids?

JANET: An eighteen-year-old daughter.

BILL: And . . . gosh, his wife?

JANET: Well, she's in India. It's not like he's really married.

BILL: Why doesn't he . . . well, just leave his wife?

JANET: He can't just do that! It's complicated!

(Still listening, Nell rolls her eyes at this.)

NELL: *(Setting down the glass.)* Ice water, lightly iced.

JANET: Sometimes I think I should just forget him entirely. Sometimes I think if there's any chance of our never being together, it's better that I'm the one not available.

BILL: This is what I wanted to talk to you about Janet. Your availability. I think . . .

(Nell brings the avocado.)

JANET: I'm sorry, did I not mention the side of avocado should be sliced?

(Nell takes the avocado away.)

BILL: Janet. I don't have any more clients today. And the class I usually teach at the Center isn't meeting today because of the er . . . Freud convention. Do you have to get back to the Center? Or do you have time for a serious talk? Not about Greg, but about . . . our lives?

JANET: Oh Bill I forgot to tell you. I did your lifetimes!

BILL: Really? That's so sweet. I asked you so long ago, I thought you'd . . . forgotten.

JANET: I remembered. You lived in the Middle East, 5,000 years ago . . .

(*"With or Without You" switches to the aria "Nessun Dorma" from the opera* Turandot. *Janet, mesmerized, starts to hum the aria and conduct it.*)

BILL: The Middle East? Ancient times? Did I have a job there? Or — was I in The Bible? . . . Are you having a vision or something?

JANET: Miss! Miss!

NELL: (*Plunking down the avocado.*) Let me guess. The avocado. You said you wanted it sliced, but now you want it diced.

JANET: No, I . . .

NELL: You want me to take the water out of the ice.

JANET: Is that the radio?

NELL: Of course not, it's a CD. Radio stations don't switch from rock to opera. Not even W-H-O-A.

JANET: Who changed the CD?

NELL: Joey the busboy changed the CD.

JANET: May I speak with Joey the busboy?

NELL: He has a callback for *Mamma Mia*.

JANET: Do you know why he changed the CD?

NELL: Because I told him to. Look, do you ever have a really rotten day?

JANET: Oh yes! Just yesterday . . .

(*Nell finally loses it. During the following, she keeps talking even as Janet tries to interrupt.*)

NELL: Good. Because today is my turn. My college roommate's visiting, she's married a hippie and had a child and they're having free love on my couch. — So I call my boyfriend to say I'm coming over, and he says he's leaving me. He writes children's books, *The Little Happy Donkey Stories?*

JANET: Oooh, sure, I —

NELL: — And he's fallen for his illustrator. He can't help it, they were always together, always with the happy donkeys, and it just — happened.

JANET: Oh, that is so . . .

NELL: Now the phone rings and it's my grandmother, she's had a heart attack, she's going into surgery.

JANET: You know, I know someone who that . . .

NELL: After seeing her in the hospital, all laid out, I come home to my friends. They have excellent timing and an alarming amount of marijuana. The whole family got high and the landlord smelled the stuff and caught them and now he's trying to have me evicted for drug possession, he wants me out so he can raise the rent. And I don't blame him, I'd kick me out too — there's a three-year-old smoking pot in my apartment!

JANET: (*Genuinely trying to help.*) Of course there is! Mercury's in retrograde!

NELL: I'll ignore that you just said that. So I brought my two favorite discs into work, because a girl who's losing her home and her grandmother and her love needs a little music. And I was enjoying the U-2 when you started bothering me about avocados. So I thought, I'll move into my Puccini mood. That mood where nothing can bother me, where stresses are just forgotten. But then you come along again with the busboy and the radio and Mercury in retrograde, and I try, believe me I try to stay in my Giacomo Puccini mood under the circumstances but you make it very difficult!

(Pause.)

That is why I changed the CD. But it didn't exactly work, now, did it?

(Janet is moved and thrilled.)

JANET: Those are your discs?

NELL: Which part didn't you understand?

(Janet takes a deep breath.)

JANET: I think that you may be my dead husband.

NELL: Look, I admit I screwed up the ice water. But this —

JANET: Those were his discs!

NELL: I burned them on my hard drive.

JANET: *(Excited as she puts it all together.)* My husband loved *The Joshua Tree* and *Turandot.* His favorite two albums. An unusual combination. "With or Without You," his favorite song. *"Nessun Dorma"* — his favorite aria. I believe in reincarnation. I'm a past life–regression therapist. You played them together. You put ice in my water — something he did all the time. You felt my presence.

NELL: Of course I felt your presence! You're crazy!

JANET: *(Overwhelmed by the similarity.)* He used to say that too!

NELL: It's not a highly original conclusion.

(Bill turns Nell; he suddenly gets assertive.)

BILL: Listen, Miss . . . I don't know if you realize who you're talking to here! You are talking to Janet Rice, Ph.D., clinical psychologist, senior faculty member at the International Therapy Center and renowned expert on alternative modalities. She is the most highly respected past life–regression therapist in the tri-state area! I would say she is at the top of her field in the whole Northeast.

NELL: OK, Dr. Past Lives. *(Beat.)* How, exactly, could I be your dead husband?

JANET: Oh! Spirits can be exchanged. They can overlap. He died four years ago but you wouldn't need to be four to be him. His soul may have replaced the last one inside of you when it went to its next life. This is not widely understood, even in the New Age community.

NELL: Four years ago was when I went through my big Puccini phase. Coincidence.

JANET: There's no such thing as coincidence. I've told you that a million times, Neil.

NELL: The name is Nell. And that's a coincidence too.

JANET: Oh Neil! You always doubted it. And now you're living in a woman named Nell who's just like you. I can take it. I just want you to know . . . I loved you. I really did.

NELL: I loved you too. *(Beat.)* Before you sent the avocado back.

JANET: U-2. Puccini. Same old. And I bet you still listen to Fauré too.

NELL: Wait. Now this is weird. How do you know I listen to Fauré?

JANET: Erik Satie. Burgmüller. Gypsy Kings.

NELL: *(Suspicious.)* How do you know this?

(Bill is beaming at Janet.)

Yes I listen to all those guys. They make me feel . . . I'm beginning to think this is truly weird on some deep level. Is that what you want?

JANET: Yes. I think it's as far as I'll ever get with you, so yes. . . . Hey, if you think you're ready, I can tell you about your other lives.

NELL: *(Curious.)* Like what?

JANET: You were a nun, in the Middle Ages. But you were disillusioned. You were seeking salvation, but saw lots of other nuns around you were just doing P.R. You were one of those people who Capricorned out — following rules, obeying, doing everything you were supposed to . . . and then losing faith.

(Nell looks skeptical.)

You've been a doctor many times. That's why your grandmother's operation is upsetting you so much, you wish you had the tools to do it in this life yourself but you don't. It makes you feel helpless.

NELL: *(Surprised.)* Yes.

JANET: A couple of your lives were full of suffering. But you have had enormous strength, always. You're stronger than the people who hurt you, even when you seem vulnerable. Your vulnerability is a mask, it's a shield. You're made of something much tougher than they realize.

(Nell is rapt in attention.)

Sorry, I'd need more time to get more. And I'm sorry about . . . burdening you with all this. This Neil stuff. That was a special lifetime for you. You were generous and good and nothing bad ever happened to you until death came for you too early. He was a wonderful man. You were a wonderful man.

NELL: *(Quite moved.)* Um. Thank you. God, that's so sweet! Even if it's not me . . . or him . . . or me . . . *(Close to tears.)* I don't know what I'm saying, I'm going to get your tuna.

(She exits.)

JANET: *(Gazing off at Nell.)* Wow, he's really starting to open up!

(Janet and Bill stare at each other.)

I'm sorry. Where were we?

BILL: I . . . I . . . You were going to tell me who I was in the Middle East.

JANET: Oh yes. You lived there 5,000 years ago. Battle of Jericho. You were an Arab, but that's not what they called you back then. You were a Samarianite or a Marionite or something. A woman.

BILL: A woman?

JANET: You made ceramics. In a battle, a man came and broke your pottery. You picked up a shard . . . could have killed him . . . but stopped. And this man, who you didn't kill, destroyed your pottery, ruined your home, murdered your husband and children. And you regretted your whole life not killing him.

BILL: *(Fascinated.)* Wow.

JANET: You've been in that situation a lot. Refusing to aggress.

BILL: Refusing to aggress.

JANET: In wars, stopping before you're supposed to kill. Some lifetimes you spent in prison for not following the law. It's Mars in the twelfth. You just don't want to look that in the face.

BILL: And in this lifetime? What am I supposed to accomplish?

JANET: That's a very good question. That is *the* question. But I don't want to impose . . .

(Decides to impose.)

OK. I think you have an addiction to rescuing. In this life, you wanted to do that, but with limits. That's why you became a therapist.

BILL: I have to say . . . whatever this all means . . . I'm feeling a very nice sensation right now from you telling me this.

(Janet nods sagely and smiles.)

JANET: I think you mean you're "seen." You're feeling very "seen."

BILL: Yes. Very seen. You know, these are different from the lifetimes Greg gave me. He only gives the pathological ones.

JANET: He's such an Aries.

BILL: That's one way of looking at it . . . But maybe he gives the pathological lives because — *(Stopping himself.)* It's none of my business . . . *(He makes the decision.)* Yes it is. I'm not going to stand by and watch. You say I've spent lifetimes doing that? Well — that's bullshit! *(Janet is startled. Bill continues as he realizes.)* But I've certainly spent this lifetime doing that, so maybe you're onto something . . . For godsakes, ever since Neil died you've been getting involved with inappropriate men . . . and I sit with you in coffee shops and listen to you go on about them and I guess I *am* like the pathetic woman with the shards and the pottery and the regrets. I guess you're right about that. Well, I'm not going to be like that anymore! Goddamnit, there is no such thing as coincidence. And it's no coincidence that I'm the one you call and I'm the one who shows up. Give me a chance. You owe that to me. To both of us.

JANET: Wow, you . . . presented that so powerfully. That was powerful.

BILL: Thank you.

JANET: I had no idea! I'm . . . much more perceptive about otherworldly things, y'know?

BILL: I know. I know.

JANET: Bill, it's . . . It's very attractive when you're in your power.

BILL: Good.

(He leans in, pulls her toward him, and kisses her. They break apart. She looks at him. They start to kiss again. Nell enters.)

NELL: Tuna on pita with bean sprouts . . .

(She sees them kissing. Possessively.)

Hey, what's going on? Weren't we just happily married?

JANET: That was — another life.

NELL: Oops. This has a tomato, I'm sorry, I told them no tomato, I'll go back and . . .

JANET: No, it's all right. Just . . . leave it.

NELL: *(Surprised.)* Sure.

(She smiles.)

Enjoy.

(Nell exits. Lights fade as Janet and Bill kiss and sounds of the aria swell.)

END OF PLAY

The Perfect Proposal

LAURA COTTON

The Perfect Proposal was originally produced on December 9, 2006, at Florida State University in an evening of ten-minute plays. The cast was as follows: David — Joele Davis, Shannon — Brenda Scott, Melissa — Donna Cross.

CHARACTERS

DAVID: mid to late twenties. A shy, nerdy guy, especially around females. He's been dating Melissa for eight months now.

SHANNON: early twenties, David's best friend. Sharp, clever, easily excited. Has a huge crush on David, but has never told him. Always thought she'd wait for a better time.

MELISSA: David's girlfriend. A queen-of-the-world type.

SETTING

David's kitchen

TIME

Present day, around six o'clock

• • •

David's kitchen. The table is beautifully set. A perfectly cooked lobster in the center. Champagne glasses and a wine bottle on the table. Chopin plays from a CD player. The lights are dimmed. At Rise: David sits at the table, on the phone.

DAVID: But we had plans. I made dinner, this was supposed to be our special . . . What? . . . No, no, I still can't hear you . . . That music, you know, it kinda sounds like . . . David Bowie! Are you at David Bowie's house? . . . Oh, a concert. But why didn't you tell me you were going to . . . Yeah, sure, we can talk about this later.

(Hangs up the phone. Pours a glass of wine and drinks it. He sits there, listening to the Chopin, a glum look on his face. The doorbell rings. He opens the door. Shannon stands before him, drenched. Her hair is soaked, her clothes and jacket are wrinkled. A large canvas bag over her shoulder.)

SHANNON: David! David! Is it too late? It is, isn't it? Isn't it?

DAVID: Too late for what?

SHANNON: Oh, David, please, please don't play with me. Your mother called an hour ago and told me, told me that you were gonna ask Melissa to marry you. Tonight! I left work early, ran down eight blocks and nearly got hit by a Hershey's truck. And then, then it started raining. Why didn't you tell me you were gonna propose?

DAVID: I was afraid you'd . . . try to talk me out of it. I know you don't like Melissa and . . .

SHANNON: We've been friends for five years, you and me. Five years. I love you like a . . . a . . . I don't know . . . like a someone. And you don't tell me! So what'd she say? After you asked her, I mean?

DAVID: Actually, I didn't. She canceled on me.

SHANNON: Then I'm not . . . I'm not too late?

DAVID: Too late for what?

SHANNON: For the . . . um . . . proposal planning. You have to plan your proposal. It's very important.

DAVID: Yeah, I know, I know. I worked it all out. I cooked her a lobster dinner,

(Motions toward the lobster.)

bought her a ring,

(Pats his shirt pocket.)

and put together a compilation of "romantic" music.

(Directs his gaze toward the CD player.)

I even got myself a knee pad,

(Rolls up his pants to reveal a knee pad on his knee.)

so that I could easily get down on one knee and ask her.

SHANNON: A knee pad. A knee pad?

DAVID: I have bad knees.

SHANNON: Mmmm . . . So Melissa's definitely not coming over?

DAVID: Definitely not.

SHANNON: Good.

(She turns the lights onto their full power, turns off the music, grabs a lobster stick, breaks the shell off, and munches on it.)

DAVID: What are you doing?!

SHANNON: I'm saving you . . . from . . . the biggest . . . mistake of your life.

DAVID: Huh?

SHANNON: How do I put this nicely? . . . Your proposal sucks, David. It's unoriginal, unexciting, and to be honest, a bit on the . . . smelly side.

DAVID: Oh . . . Really?

SHANNON: Yes.

DAVID: Uh . . . OK. How would you . . . I mean, how do you think I should ask her?

SHANNON: Well, there are five types of proposals, David. But you probably already knew that . . .

DAVID: Actually, I didn't.

SHANNON: Well, there are. There's the adventurous proposal, the romantic proposal, the so-casual-you-don't-know-it's-happening proposal, the sexy proposal, and of course, the ultimatum proposal. But that one is usually reserved for women and only to be used in the most dire of emergencies.

DAVID: Should I be taking notes?

SHANNON: Yes.

DAVID: I was joking.

SHANNON: I wasn't.

(Grabs a pen and paper out of her bag, hands it to David.)

Let's start with the adventurous proposal. Imagine this. You're taking Melissa hiking through the woods. Now, as we walk you're gonna pretend I'm Melissa. And at some point you should ask me to marry you. OK?

DAVID: Uh, sure . . .

(Shannon opens her bag, takes out a CD. Puts it in the CD player. The sounds of nature play. She also takes out two foldable walking sticks and two safari type hats. She puts one hat on, puts the other on David's head, and hands one of the walking sticks to him. David stares at her, curiously.)

DAVID: *(Continued.)* This is weird. Do you always carry around . . .

SHANNON: No time for talking. OK. I'm Melissa now. Ready, set, go!

(She walks through the kitchen, using the hiking stick. David watches, bewildered.)

SHANNON: Me o' my o, me o' my o'! It's a beautiful day today, isn't it, David?

DAVID: It's not day, it's night, and . . .

SHANNON: We're *pretending*, David. Remember?

DAVID: Oh right. Right . . .

(Walks a little, uses the hiking stick.)

It is a beautiful day, Shannon.

SHANNON: Melissa.

DAVID: What about her?

SHANNON: I'm Melissa.

DAVID: No, you're not.

SHANNON: *Pretending*, David. *Pretending*.

DAVID: Oh, right. Right. Sorry. It *is* a beautiful day, Melissa.

SHANNON: Don't you think I look beautiful too?

DAVID: Yes, *you* are beautiful. Nature *is* beautiful. Everything, *Melissa*, is beautiful.

SHANNON: Oh my God! Oh my God!

DAVID: What? What's wrong?

SHANNON: There's a bug on me!

DAVID: What? Where?

SHANNON: You can't see it! It's a tick. I can just feel it. It's crawling, crawling all over me!

Get it off! Get it off of me!

DAVID: How can I if I don't see it?

SHANNON: Just kill it! Kill it, you sissy man! OK. Enough a' that. Now you see why the adventurous proposal is not always successful.

DAVID: Wait. Are you saying there really wasn't a bug on you?

SHANNON: Of course not. I said, *several* times, that we were just pretending.

DAVID: Oh. Right. I knew that.

SHANNON: Moving on. The romantic proposal. Imagine this. You ask Melissa to marry you after a full night of . . . tango dancing!

DAVID: I can't tango dance. I can barely . . . regular dance.

SHANNON: That's OK. Just follow my lead. And at some point, ask me to marry you.

(Shannon takes a CD out of her bag, puts it in David's CD player. Tango music comes on. Then She takes David's hands and begins to lead Him through the tango. He does the woman's part, She does the man's. At the end of the dance, Shannon dips David. It looks ridiculous.)

SHANNON: Now, David! Ask me now.

DAVID: OK, OK . . . Will you . . . marry me, Melissa?

(Shannon drops David, causing him to fall out of the dip.)

SHANNON: Sure, I'll marry you.

DAVID: Really?

SHANNON: Right after you learn to dance.

(Shannon turns off the music.)

SHANNON: I'm just gonna say it. The romantic proposal isn't for you. Don't even think about it.

DAVID: I tried to tell you I couldn't d . . .

SHANNON: Let's move onto the-so-casual-you-don't-realize-it's-happening proposal. You and Melissa are at the gym.

(She takes another CD out of her bag. Puts it in the player. Fast-paced techno music plays.)

You're running . . . Well, run, already David!

(David jogs in place.)

SHANNON: *(Continued.)* Melissa's on the floor doing sit-ups.

(Sits down, does sit-ups on the floor.)

Now, we're gonna talk and at some time, during our conversation, you're gonna ask me to marry you. Real casual, like it's no big deal.

DAVID: OK . . . So Melissa . . . you're really . . . working that tummy a' yours.

SHANNON: You think I have a tummy?!

DAVID: Well, what I mean is . . .

SHANNON: You never mentioned a tummy before!

DAVID: Everybody has a tummy. Listen, Melissa, I've been thinking . . . and I think we should, you know, do what other people do.

SHANNON: Have wild sex?

DAVID: Well, yeah, I'd love that too, but . . .

SHANNON: 'Cause it's not happening. Never again. Not after what you just said about my tummy.

DAVID: What?

SHANNON: OK. Enough. You're not exactly doing well here, David. You know that, don't you?

DAVID: I'm doing the best I can! Your sex comment, it distracted me.

SHANNON: Speaking of sex, let's move on to . . . the sexy engagement.
(Dims the lights, then takes another CD out of her bag. Puts it in the CD player. Slow jazz music plays. She strips down to a sexy blue baby doll. Dances seductively.)

DAVID: Uh . . . I feel kinda weird about this. I mean, I appreciate your efforts but . . .

SHANNON: David, if you want to have the perfect proposal you need to practice. Think of this. You're in the mood. But Melissa . . . she's . . . Melissa. A cold fish, as your mother calls her. So it's up to you. You have to seduce her. How about giving me . . . I mean . . . Melissa a massage?

DAVID: But Melissa doesn't . . .

SHANNON: Please, David. Just do it.
(David nods, walks over to Shannon, starts massaging her back.)

SHANNON: *(Continued.)* Wow. That feels really good . . . Do you . . . do this to Melissa a lot?

DAVID: Are you kidding? Melissa would kill me! She hates it when people touch her.

SHANNON: Hates it when people touch . . . why do you want to marry her?

DAVID: Why? Well . . . I've been with her for eight months. That's the longest relationship she's ever had. And all she talks about now is how all her friends are getting married. It's time, she says. It's time for me to ask her.

SHANNON: David, David, David, David. Are you in love with her?

DAVID: Well, she's not my dream girl.
(Beat.)
But I'd never get my dream girl.

SHANNON: David, I need to tell you something.

(Beat.)

I have always —

MELISSA: Well, lookie what we have here!

(Goes to the CD player, turns off the music.)

DAVID AND SHANNON: Melissa!

DAVID: What are you doing here?

MELISSA: I left the concert right after you called. The guy beside me was like totally hitting on me. He kept trying to touch my knee. And you know how I am about people touching me!

(Glares at David.)

I didn't think you were the type to cheat, David.

SHANNON: We were just practicing. David was trying to figure out how he should . . .

DAVID: Propose to you.

MELISSA: Yeah, right.

SHANNON: He really was.

MELISSA: *(To David.)* OK, so do it.

DAVID: What?

MELISSA: Propose to me. Now. Right now.

SHANNON: The ultimatum proposal.

DAVID: I don't think *now* is a good —

MELISSA: Ask me!

DAVID: No.

MELISSA: What?

DAVID: I'm not asking you. I don't even know why I was thinking of asking you.

MELISSA: Well, I wouldn't have said yes anyway.

DAVID: Good.

MELISSA: Good?! Are you crazy? Are you out of your mind?

DAVID: Melissa, you know we aren't right for each other, you know —

MELISSA: David. Please. Don't do this. You don't have to marry me right this minute. We could wait a few days.

DAVID: No. I'm not going to marry you. Not now, not tomorrow, not ever. It's over, Melissa. It's completely over.

MELISSA: But David it could be different, I could be different, *we* could be —

DAVID: No.

MELISSA: You'll never find anyone like me. Never!

(Storms out of the room.)

DAVID: That's the point.

(Melissa leaves, slamming the door behind her.)

SHANNON: I'm sorry, David. This is all my fault.

DAVID: No.

SHANNON: Yes.

DAVID: No.

SHANNON: Yes.

DAVID: Yes.

SHANNON: No.

(David and Shannon look at each other and burst out laughing.)

SHANNON: Look, I was trying to tell you this earlier. The thing is I . . . I would never want to do anything that could in any way jeopardize our friendship but . . .

DAVID: What?

SHANNON: Do you want to go out sometime? On a date, I mean?

DAVID: What kind of date?

SHANNON: What *kind* of date?

DAVID: Yeah. You know, there are seven kinds of dates. There's the, "I like him, but I don't love him date," the "I just want to sleep with him date," the "we're just friends date," the "double date," the . . .

(Shannon laughs as Lights Fade.)

END OF PLAY

Playthings

MARK SAUNDERS

Playthings was first produced by Heartland Theatre Company, Bloomington, Ill., at The Attic Plays, Heartland's Annual 10-Minute Play Festival on June 9–26, 2005. Director: Wade Hicks. The cast: Joe — Scott Hogan, Babs — Alexis Wood, Teddy — Sarah Torbeck. Other productions: Theatre One Productions, Middleboro, Massachusetts, A Slice of Life (festival of short plays), February 2006. Director: Peg Holzemer. Cast: Joe — Jeff Rebell, Babs — Patricia Minkle, Teddy — Richard Pacheco. The Alliance Theatre Company, Burbank, California Anniversary Festival on August, 2006. Director: Dawn Zeek. Joe — Darrell Bryan, Teddy — Bryan Kopta, Babs — Dawn Zeek.

CHARACTERS

    JOE: a male action figure dressed in military fatigues

    BABS: a female fashion model, a "doll" dressed in pink

    TEDDY: either male or female, cute and cuddly, with a furry coat and
        "teddy bear" ears

SETTING

    The attic of a suburban home

TIME

    Daytime

•   •   •

*Notes: One late afternoon in an unfinished room with exposed beams and a
small window. Typical attic. Closed boxes of stuff scattered around the stage.
A door to one side of the stage; a tiny oval window at the opposite end. Three
figures stand inside a cardboard box. Each wear large circular stickers marked
ten cents. The box is cut low, so the sides rise slightly above their ankles. Joe
mimics pointing a rifle. Babs remains stiff, her arms close to her body, fists
slightly open. Teddy's arms extend out as if appealing to be picked up and held.
All three stand frozen for several beats. A door slams shut offstage. A couple of
beats. Then, Joe springs into action. He jumps out of the box and looks offstage, in the direction of the shut door. He turns to face the others.*

JOE: I don't believe it. I friggin' don't believe it.

    (Babs steps out of the box and wags her finger at Joe.)

BABS: Language.

JOE: Language yourself. You don't get it do you? Why am I talking to you?
    You never get anything.

TEDDY: Why are you always so mean to her?

JOE: I call them as I see them.

TEDDY: Yeah, well, who died and made you king of the universe?

JOE: I know what I know.

    *(Teddy jumps out of the box, walks over to Babs and puts an arm around
    her.)*

TEDDY: That's OK, Babs. Joe didn't mean anything by it.

BABS: What'd he say?

    (Teddy shrugs and walks away.)

JOE: *(Addresses Teddy.)* Tell me at least you understand, Teddy. You heard what they said. You know what's going on.

TEDDY: I think so. They're having a garage sale tomorrow.

(Babs rubs her hands and runs around excited.)

BABS: A sale! I love sales. I hope they have shoes. It's been so long since I've shopped for shoes. I can't wait. Oh boy. Oh boy. Oh boy. Now, what to wear. Let's see.

JOE: You bimbo. We're not going to shop for anything. We're going to be sold.

BABS: Sold?

JOE: Yes. Sold. S-O-L-D. As in out of here. Gone. Kaput. Sayonara. What's worse, if no one buys us, they're sending us to the city dump.

BABS: Dump?

JOE: As in garbage. Thrown away. Disposed of. Shit-canned. *(Waves his hand and sits on a box.)* I give up. Explain it to her.

(Teddy walks up to Babs and looks her in the eye.)

TEDDY: What Joe is trying to say is. Well. You see. They've been watching those home remodel shows, you know, a lot of them, and now they want to redo the attic. Update it, especially now that the kids are gone to college. Everyone's doing it. So, it's nothing personal but they need to get rid of a lot of their old ju —

JOE: — I wouldn't go there.

(Joe stands and paces.)

BABS: Go where?

TEDDY: They need to make room for the remodel, you know. So, they have to sell some of their things. Ergo, tomorrow they're having a garage sale. And there's a chance we'll all be sold to someone else.

BABS: Sold? *(Beat before it sinks in and she sits.)* Sold.

(Joe walks up to Babs and points to the sticker on her chest.)

JOE: What do you think that thing is, a designer logo?

(Babs reads the sticker for the first time.)

BABS: Ten cents?

JOE: One tenth of a dollar.

TEDDY: Two nickels.

(Babs jumps to her feet.)

BABS: TEN CENTS! I've been discounted! They're going to sell me for a lousy dime! How dare they discount me? Why I. I. I. I invented dress up!

JOE: And that's if you're lucky. Nobody buys you and — Kreeeech!

(Joe mimics having his own throat cut.)

(Babs sits.)

BABS: Ohhh. They wouldn't.

JOE: Ya think? They do it all the time. No advance warning. No severance. Career counseling? Job retraining? Forget about it.

TEDDY: As usual, you're over-reacting. All testosterone and no brain cells. Think it through, man. Someone will want us. Have faith.

JOE: You know the difference between garage and garbage? *(Beat.)* The letter *B*.

TEDDY: Would it hurt you to think good thoughts for once? Look at us. We're American classics. Someone is bound to buy us all.

BABS: I hope you're right.

TEDDY: Absolutely. We'll be picked up in the first hour. Mark my words.

JOE: That's easy for you to say. You're cuddly. But we're both action figures. We go back on the market and suddenly we're competing against multi-media, 3-D video programs. Game Boys. iPods. Photo-taking mobile phones. Not to mention a hundred or so cable shows on TV. CDs. DVDs. All those cheap, foreign whiz-bang electronics. And what do I have? Twenty-one movable parts. Manually movable, mind you.

BABS: Speak for yourself. I have my own line of fashionable clothes and accessories. I'm a real catch.

JOE: Catch? Now my cousin Leo. There's a catch. I should have gone into his line of work.

TEDDY: What's he do?

JOE: He's an adult toy.

BABS: Adult toy? Toys are for kids.

JOE: Not these toys. They're marital aids.

BABS: You silly men. What's a toy have to do with marriage?

(Joe leans in and whispers into Babs' ear. She reacts in horror.)

BABS: *(Deep voice.)* THAT'S DISGUSTING!

JOE: You do what you have to do to survive. Least ways he's working.

TEDDY: *(Giggles.)* Hard at it. I'd say.

JOE: *(Laughs.)* Lucky stiff.

TEDDY: It's a growth market.

BABS: Wait a minute? This isn't right. We can't be thrown away. Don't I have something to say about this? I'm too young to be disposed of just like that. Without any say. I mean. I'm just getting started. Why, I haven't even had kids yet. I want children.

JOE: You're a doll.

BABS: Thank you.

JOE: No, I mean you are a doll. You can't have kids.

(Babs prances around, showing off her figure.)

BABS: Yeah, right. Think again, bucko. Just check out this bod. I'm hot. I'm the original stud magnet.

TEDDY: 'Fraid he's right. No kids. You're a doll. Look at the bright side. You can eat whatever you want and never put on weight.

BABS: Hmmmm. I can work with that.

TEDDY: Maybe we could team up. Do something together. Something different, you know.

JOE: You mean, pool our talents and take charge of our own careers, be retrained and all that? Might work.

BABS: If you're thinking adult toy, forget about it.

(Joe jumps up on a box.)

JOE: I'm not forgetting about any of this. Are you ready to throw in the towel? Are we going to stand idly by and let impersonal contraptions and electronic gadgetry take our rightful place?

TEDDY / BABS: No!

JOE: Is it fair to lose out to foreign competition, to a cheaper product made without environmental protection guarantees or product-testing assurances?

TEDDY / BABS: No!

JOE: After so many years of loyal service, is it fair to have to settle for so much less? To live without a social safety net?

TEDDY / BABS: No!

JOE: Are you ready to be displaced without a fight? Are you ready to be thrown away?

TEDDY / BABS: No!

JOE: If you prick me, do I not bleed?

(Teddy and Babs turn to stare at each other before responding in unison.)

BABS / TEDDY: No!

JOE: Join me now and we'll take charge of our own destiny. Join me now and we'll charge out of this room, together, as a team. All for one and one for all. Together we stand, in victory. Toys of America, Unite! Follow me. To the outside.

(Joe runs to the tiny oval window at the other side of the stage, across from the door. Teddy and Babs follow him. A few beats as they stare out the window. Then, Joe turns away, walks to a box. Teddy turns to watch him while Babs still looks out the window. Joe sits.)

JOE: A soldier. A fashion model. And a teddy bear. What are we supposed to do? Become the next Village People? There's no way out. We are already what we do best. And the world's passing us by. The simple truth is, we no longer contribute.

(Teddy tiptoes closer to the stairs and tilts his head to listen.)

TEDDY: Wait a minute. Something's going on downstairs.

(Babs walks over to where Joe sits.)

TEDDY: Little Johnny's back from college. He's arguing with his parents about something. It seems. Yes. You go, boy.

BABS: What? What's going on. Tell me. Please. Tell me.

TEDDY: *(Turns to Babs.)* We're going to be recycled.

BABS: Oh, my God! Recycled?

(Joe stands, re-energized. He runs to the door and listens.)

JOE: Ooh Rah! Recycled.

BABS: *(Starts to cry.)* I don't want to be recycled. That sounds so awful. Does it hurt?

JOE: No. No. It's a good thing. Trust me. Being recycled is a good thing. A very good thing. It means someone somewhere still needs us. We probably won't be together. And we'll most likely be moving into a lower economic income category.

BABS: What's that?

TEDDY: A poorer household.

BABS: *(Dejected.)* Hand me downs.

JOE: Sure, we might not be as appreciated as before. But at least we'll be working.

(A door slams.)

BABS: Yea!!! We're not disposables. We're recyclables. Do we still get to go to the sale?

JOE: We live to work and play another day. Quiet. I hear the door. They're coming back. If I don't get a chance to tell you this, you're the best group of toys a guy could ever hope to lead in battle.

BABS: What battle?

TEDDY: Play along. It's all he knows.

JOE: It's been great working with you both. I'll miss you.

BABS: And I'll miss you guys, you big galoots.

(Teddy sticks his arms out to the others.)

TEDDY: Group hug.

(They pull together and hug each other for a beat. Then, Joe pulls away.)

JOE: Places everyone. Back to work.

(They jump back inside the cardboard box and assume their original positions.)

(Lights fade slowly into darkness.)

END OF PLAY

Surprise

Mark Harvey Levine

Surprise was first produced by Theatre Neo (Los Angeles) as part of *Open All Night* in May 2000. It was directed by Loren E. Chadima, with the following cast: Whitney — Carolyn Hennesy, Peter — Mark Harvey Levine, Esther — Sarah Nina Phillips. *Surprise* had its first Equity production as part of *Cabfare for the Common Man* at The Phoenix Theatre (Indianapolis) in May 2005. Bryan D. Fonseca is the artistic director. It was directed by Bryan D. Fonseca, with the following cast: Whitney — Sara Rieman, Peter — Jon Lindley, Esther — Deborah Sargent.

CHARACTERS

WHITNEY: very well put together, nicely dressed
PETER: a bit of a sad sack, rumpled
ESTHER: the very capable waitress

SETTING

A cheap, all-night diner

•   •   •

A cheap, all-night diner. Peter studies his menu sheepishly. Whitney, much better put together, does not look at her menu, but stares at him, steaming mad.

WHITNEY: Well, that's another evening thoroughly —
PETER: — ruined. I'm sorry, Whitney. Please don't —
WHITNEY: I can never see Jane and Margaret again. My only lesbian friends! I've lost my lesbians!
PETER: You haven't lost —
WHITNEY: I've never felt so —
PETER: — embarrassed, I know —
WHITNEY: *(Overlapping.)* — embarrassed in all my — Stop that! I hate when you—
PETER: — finish your sentences, I'm sorry.
WHITNEY: *(Overlapping.)* — finish my — ! Yes!
PETER: I can't help it. You know I'm psychic.
WHITNEY: Yes, I know you're psychic, Peter. Everyone knows you're psychic. Jane and Margaret know you're psychic. Anyone forgets, wait five minutes, you'll remind them.
PETER: I knew you wouldn't understand.
WHITNEY: Ha ha. Very funny. God! You're not even an INTERESTING psychic. No, you're the ONE guy who's only psychic two minutes ahead.
PETER: I'm sorry. Are you ready to order?
(As if on cue, Esther, the waitress, arrives at this moment.)
ESTHER: Are you ready to order? Oh hi, Peter.
WHITNEY: Does SHE know you're psychic? He's psychic, y'know.
ESTHER: I know.
PETER: I always come here when I'm about to be dumped. *(To Esther.)* I'll have the usual.

WHITNEY: — Dumped?!

PETER: And she'll have the blueberry Belgian waffles. And we both want coffee.

WHITNEY: I'll order for myself, thank you very much.

(Whitney grabs the menu, looks it over for a long beat.)

WHITNEY: *(Continued.)* I want the waffles. *(To Peter.)* Damn you, damn you.

ESTHER: I'll be back with your coffee.

(Esther exits.)

WHITNEY: So you know I'm going to dump you?

PETER: It's pretty obvious.

WHITNEY: — In the next two minutes?!

PETER: No . . . I think I've always known this day would come.

WHITNEY: We've only been dating three weeks.

PETER: Please don't break up with me, Whitney! I can't help myself! It's not easy being psychic! I had a terrible childhood.

(Esther arrives with two cups of coffee as he speaks.)

PETER: *(Continued.)* When Jimmy DeFornick would beat me up, I could feel each punch before it landed. Sometimes — you're going to burn your mouth — if I knew he was going to break my glasses I'd take them off and break them myself.

(As Peter speaks, Whitney defiantly gulps her coffee and holds it in her bulging cheeks, glaring at him. Her mouth is frying.)

PETER: *(Continued.) (Without pausing.)* He found that amusing. And I knew he would.

(Whitney swallows, speaking funny at first due to her burnt mouth.)

WHITNEY: Look, we all had louthy childhoodth, OK? Stacey Gerber used to stomp on my toes during baton practice. It doesn't give you the —

PETER: — I didn't!

WHITNEY: LET ME FINISH! Just once, just once in the final moments of this relationship, I would like to finish a sentence. Thank you. *(Pause, fuming.)* I forgot what I was going to —

PETER: "— the right to pick fights with your —"

WHITNEY: *(Overlapping.)* — with my friends! Yes!

PETER: *(Overlapping.)* And then I say "I didn't," and you say —

PETER AND WHITNEY: *(Simultaneously.)* You most certainly did.

PETER: *(Continued.)* — And then I say —

WHITNEY: Stop that!

PETER: — And it's all so boring.

WHITNEY: Don't say things along with me!

PETER: Why bother having the fight if — ?

WHITNEY: You know I hate that!

PETER: All I said to them was the Spinach Mushroom Lasagna was going to be dry and inedib —

WHITNEY: — They MADE the Spinach Mushroom Las —

PETER: — How was I supposed to kn — ?

WHITNEY: *(Banging table.)* — BECAUSE YOU'RE PSYCHIC!!

PETER: Look, I only know the next two minutes, OK? I can't tell who made dinner. I'm not a food-psychic. Except ours is here.

(Right on cue, Esther enters with their food: waffles for Whitney and a bowl of cornflakes for Peter.)

ESTHER: Here ya go! Blueberry Belgian Waffles, and one "I'm Getting Dumped" Special.

WHITNEY: Cornflakes?! You go to a restaurant and order cornflakes?!

PETER: *(Meekly.)* I like how they do them here.

ESTHER: Can I get you anything else?

PETER: We're fine. Just bring the towel.

(Esther exits.)

PETER: *(Continued.)* And the lasagna WAS dry and inedi —

WHITNEY: Of course it was! It always is! It's their specialty! That's why you go out to eat afterwards! And you don't have to be psychic to know when someone invites you over, they made the damn dinner!

PETER: I don't get invited over too much.

WHITNEY: Can't imagine why.

PETER: Well, people get freaked out just because I —

WHITNEY: Sarcasm! That was sarcasm! You know what? I want to thank you. I do. You've taught me the true meaning of hate. Oh, I thought I'd hated before. But I realize now it was a mere youthful dislike. Puppy hate. But with you, I finally know what it means to hate someone! I detest you with a passion I've never felt before! I despise you! I abhor you! Why, I think I loathe you! *(Pause.)* God, I hate you!

PETER: Doesn't surprise me.

WHITNEY: Agggggggggghhhh!!!

PETER: You missed.

(She throws a waffle at him, missing him of course.)

WHITNEY: AGGGGGGGGGGGGGGGGGGGGGGGHHHH!!!

(She throws her water at him, hitting him full in the face — precisely as Esther arrives with a towel. Peter dries off and tosses the towel to Esther, who

catches it one-handed, hardly looking, as she passes by. They've obviously done this before.)

WHITNEY: *(With great, but unsteady, calmness.)* Well. I think it is obvious that we are through, here, Peter. I feel no need to stay. *(To Esther.)* Could you bring us the —

ESTHER: — check?

WHITNEY: *(Going to pieces.)* — Let me say it!!! LET ME SAY IT!!! Check!!! Check check check!!! In fact, never mind! He's going to pay! *(To Peter.)* But then you knew that, didn't you?!

(Esther holds the door open for Whitney as she storms out.)

PETER: *(To himself.)* Watch your step.

(We hear a crash and a distant "Dammit!!" from Whitney, offstage.)

PETER: *(Continued.)* *(Sadly, to Esther.)* She was too good for me.

ESTHER: Are you kidding me? Honey, I've seen you get dumped by a lot of women, and she was definitely the worst of 'em.

PETER: She was my last chance. I'm never gonna f —

ESTHER: You'll find someone. You'll see. Someone pretty, smart, independent . . . who won't mind that you order cornflakes.

PETER: What are you, psy — ?

ESTHER: *(Overlapping.)* — Psychic? Nah. Let's just call it a hunch.

(She grabs him and kisses him, full on the mouth. Peter stands stunned for a moment.)

PETER: . . . Didn't see THAT coming . . .

ESTHER: Surprise!

PETER: But . . . Why didn't I know? Why couldn't I — ?

ESTHER: — tell? I guess some things even a psychic can't see.

PETER: Hey — you finished one of my —

ESTHER: — sentences. Do you —

PETER: — mind? No. No, I don't. So what happens —

ESTHER: — next?

PETER AND ESTHER: *(Simultaneously.)* *(Smiling.)* I don't know . . . !

(Blackout.)

END OF PLAY

Table for Three

CARL L. WILLIAMS

Produced by Phare Play Productions, Producers Club,
New York City, November 17–19, 2006, as part of *Inside Carl's
Shorts*, an evening of one-acts. Directed by Casey Duncan with
the following cast: Beeker — Mayank Saxena, Jennifer —
Jasmine Spiess, Roy — Tim Kondrat. Also produced in
Pan Theater's Ten Minute Play Festival, San Francisco and
Snowdance 10 Minute Play Festival, Racine, Wisc.,
by Over Our Head Players.

CHARACTERS

    BEEKER: meek and solitary diner

    JENNIFER: attractive woman of mystery

    ROY: a jealous tough guy

SETTING

    Restaurant patio, one table

TIME

    Present, evening

• • •

(At Rise: Beeker is seated by himself, looking at a menu. Jennifer enters, glances behind her nervously, sees Beeker and comes over.)

JENNIFER: Excuse me . . . would you mind if I join you? *(Sits down.)*

BEEKER: What? Wait . . . I don't know.

JENNIFER: Just for a moment. Please.

BEEKER: Who are you?

JENNIFER: My name is Jennifer, and I'm in terrible trouble. *(Looks around fearfully.)*

BEEKER: What kind of trouble?

JENNIFER: I was supposed to meet someone here tonight . . . a man. But my husband found out about it.

BEEKER: Your husband?

JENNIFER: He followed me here. Luckily, I was able to reach my friend on his cell phone and warn him away.

BEEKER: Look, I really don't understand —

JENNIFER: My husband is horribly jealous. There's no telling what he might do if he caught me with another man.

BEEKER: *(Alarmed.)* So you sat here?

JENNIFER: Roy has a furious temper, and I'm really afraid of him. You'll protect me, won't you?

BEEKER: Me?

JENNIFER: Maybe he won't see us out here on the patio. The restaurant is so crowded inside.

BEEKER: Now listen here, you better get up and leave before he —

JENNIFER: Too late.

(Roy enters, looks around angrily. She tries to hide her face, but He spots her and strides over.)

JENNIFER: Oh, no — here he comes.

ROY: There you are!

JENNIFER: Roy!

ROY: I knew you were cheating on me.

JENNIFER: It's not what you think.

BEEKER: No, it's not what you think.

ROY: Shut up, you little creep.

BEEKER: Creep! See here!

ROY: I can't believe you're two-timing me with him.

JENNIFER: If you'd let me explain —

ROY: All the years we've been together, and it comes to this. How could you do this to me?

JENNIFER: I didn't want to, Roy. But you haven't been giving me what I need the most. Affection.

ROY: And he has?

BEEKER: No, I haven't! I don't even know her.

ROY: What a weasel. I wondered who it was I'd find you with. What's your name, weasel?

BEEKER: My name is Beeker, and I've never seen this woman before in my life.

JENNIFER: Oh, Beeker darling, how can you say that? After all we've meant to each other?

BEEKER: What?! You don't mean anything to me.

ROY: You're not just a weasel, you're a rat.

BEEKER: I won't sit here and be talked to like that.

ROY: Then why don't you get out of here? While you still can.

JENNIFER: Maybe it would be better.

BEEKER: I'm not leaving! I haven't even ordered yet. You're the ones who are leaving!

JENNIFER: Now, Beeker, don't make a scene.

BEEKER: *(Looks around.)* Waiter! Where's that waiter?

JENNIFER: Service here was always slow.

ROY: So you've been here before! With him, or somebody else?

JENNIFER: Beeker's the first. Honest.

BEEKER: I'm the — ? Waiter!

ROY: Calling the waiter won't do you any good. Not when I get through with you.

JENNIFER: Please, Roy — don't. Not his fingers.

BEEKER: My fingers?

JENNIFER: Roy does fingers for the people he works for.

ROY: When somebody doesn't pay up. *(Squeezes one hand with the other.)*

BEEKER: You mean you're a — you're a —

ROY: I'm a what?

BEEKER: I don't know!

JENNIFER: He hurts people for a living.

ROY: And those guys weren't messing with my wife.

BEEKER: I'm not messing with anybody!

ROY: It's always the quiet ones. But you won't be quiet much longer. *(Steps toward him.)*

BEEKER: Don't you come near me!

(Jennifer jumps up, stands behind Beeker, and lays her arms protectively across his chest.)

JENNIFER: I won't let you hurt him.

ROY: Move away, Jennifer.

JENNIFER: Not while you're this angry.

ROY: You don't think I have a right to be angry?

JENNIFER: It's not about rights. It's about the way we feel.

ROY: I feel angry!

JENNIFER: You can't blame us for falling in love.

BEEKER: We're not in love! *(Grabs her arms and pulls them away.)*

ROY: You'll get over him when he's gone.

(Roy advances, and Beeker pulls her arms back over him.)

BEEKER: There are laws, you know. What you're wanting to do is wrong.

ROY: I never let that stop me. Just like it didn't stop the two of you.

JENNIFER: You're right. We shouldn't have given in to our emotions.

ROY: You're my wife, Jennifer. Doesn't that mean anything?

JENNIFER: *(Moves away from Beeker.)* Of course it does. But I didn't know if it still meant anything to you.

ROY: I wouldn't be here if it didn't.

JENNIFER: Beeker, dear . . . perhaps we've been acting foolishly. We were too rash, too impetuous in our passion.

BEEKER: What passion? There's no passion!

JENNIFER: All those mad nights of lovemaking . . . lying in each other's arms . . . giving our bodies to each other . . . hour, after hour, after hour.

ROY: I can't take this. I just gotta break something.

(Roy moves forward. Beeker sticks his hands deep in his armpits.)

BEEKER: No!

JENNIFER: Wait. Breaking things isn't the answer.

ROY: Yeah? Then why did you break my heart?

JENNIFER: I never meant to hurt you. It was just a harmless affair. Isn't that right, Beeker?

BEEKER: Yes . . . I mean no. Harmless — yes.

JENNIFER: In fact, we were calling it off tonight.

ROY: I wish I could believe you.

BEEKER: Me, too.

JENNIFER: Roy, we need to sit down and talk this through.

BEEKER: That's good! Go somewhere and talk!

ROY: I'm not going anywhere till we get this straight.

JENNIFER: Very well, then. We'll settle it right here. *(Sits down.)*

BEEKER: I'm having dinner here!

JENNIFER: You said yourself you hadn't ordered yet. And I hardly see how we can have dinner together now. Sit down, Roy. *(Gestures to a chair.)*

ROY: I hope this won't take too long. I have work to do. *(Glares at Beeker, sits down.)*

JENNIFER: That's part of the problem. You been put all your energy into your work, with no time for me.

ROY: I make time for you.

JENNIFER: Oh, sure. When you come home late and ask me to bandage your knuckles.

ROY: A man needs a little sympathy after a tough day on the job.

JENNIFER: But we never go out together anymore. The only place you take me is for granted.

ROY: Is that why you went out with . . . him?

JENNIFER: Now, don't pick on Beeker. He's been a sweetheart.

ROY: Your sweetheart.

BEEKER: I wish you'd leave me out of this. Just leave me alone — both of you.

ROY: How can I leave you alone when you're sitting here with my wife?

JENNIFER: He has a point, Beeker. Maybe Roy and I should be by ourselves. Would you mind?

BEEKER: You mean — ? Where am I supposed to have dinner?

JENNIFER: *(Looking.)* There's a nice place across the street.

BEEKER: That's a taco stand!

JENNIFER: They have those cute little stools.

ROY: And the best part is, you'll still have fingers to eat your taco with.

BEEKER: *(Grudgingly.)* All I wanted was a quiet dinner out. *(Gets up.)*

JENNIFER: Thank you so much, Beeker . . . for everything.

ROY: Hey.

BEEKER: She didn't mean that.

JENNIFER: Take care of yourself.

ROY: Shake hands? *(Stretches out a hand.)*

BEEKER: *(Jumps back.)* No! No offense.

> *(Beeker exits. Jennifer and Roy lovingly take hold of each other's hands across the table.)*

JENNIFER: All alone, finally.

ROY: I thought we'd never get rid of him.

JENNIFER: Were we cruel, darling?

ROY: A little. But it was worth it to get the table where I proposed to you.

JENNIFER: No other table would do, not on our anniversary.

ROY: Beeker would've been here for an hour.

JENNIFER: Poor dear. I do hope he likes tacos.

> *(Blackout.)*

END OF PLAY

Third Wheel

MONICA FLORY

Third Wheel was first produced at the Emerging Artists Theatre
(Paul Adams, Artistic Director) during Spring Eatfest 2007 on
March 14, 2007. It was directed by Ned Thorne; the set design
was by Nick Lazzaro; the costume design was by Ellen Reilly;
the lighting design was by G. Benjamin Swope; the sound
design was by Ned Thorne; the production stage manager was
Tzipora Kaplan. The cast was as follows: Ken — Eric Baker,
Barbara — Amy Howard, Lisa — Clair Tyers/Nicole Gregory.

CHARACTERS
BARBARA: early thirties, a beautiful and well-dressed lounge singer
KEN: early thirties, a handsome and well-dressed lawyer
LISA: twenties, a cute and charming stalker

SETTING
A plush wine bar

TIME
Friday night, 9 PM

.   .   .

Ken sits in a bar, looking around. He drinks wine, fixes his clothing and hair.

BARBARA: (*Enters, approaches Ken.*) Hi!

KEN: Oh, hi!

(*They do an awkward handshake-hug-kiss sequence, then sit.*)

BARBARA: Well, it's nice to see you again.

KEN: And you. I hope you don't mind — I've taken the liberty of ordering you a glass of wine.

BARBARA: I don't mind at all. Cheers!

KEN: Cheers!

(*They clink glasses.*)

BARBARA: What a great place — how did you find it?

KEN: Last week's *Time Out*. It's a new place, actually. Just opened.

BARBARA: Well, I guess we're on the cutting edge, then. Not bad.

KEN: Hey, stick with me.

BARBARA: I'm so glad you called. I had a great time last week.

KEN: I did, too. You are a very intriguing woman, Barbara. I must admit that I'm dying to hear you sing. Any chance you'll let me see one of your performances?

BARBARA: Sure, whenever you want. Just so I absolutely don't know you're there. Actually, I'm singing downtown next week. I just happen to have a promotional postcard. I hope that's not presumptuous.

KEN: Of course not. Should I stand in the back? Hide myself?

BARBARA: Yes, and please don't laugh.

KEN: I would never laugh at you.

BARBARA: No, I mean you have a very distinctive laugh.

KEN: Oh.

BARBARA: But not in a negative way! I didn't mean it in the negative sense. You have a lovely laugh.

KEN: Thank you.

BARBARA: Your laugh would give you away — that's all I meant. It's distinctive in a good way. Forgiven?

KEN: And forgotten.

(Lisa enters, spots Barbara and gazes at her.)

BARBARA: Marvelous. On to more important things. I guess you're not supposed to talk politics or religion on the second date, but here goes! Could you believe the *Times* this morning? Do you read the *Times?*

KEN: Yes. I'm sorry . . . there seems to be someone staring at us.

BARBARA: Oh, goodness, could it be? *(Looks.)* Hi, Lisa.

(Lisa waves.)

BARBARA: Sorry about that. So in the *Times* this morning . . .

KEN: Do you want to say hello?

BARBARA: Oh, I just did.

KEN: Do you want to take a moment to talk to her? I don't mind.

BARBARA: No, that's OK. Thanks. Anyway, as I was saying . . .

KEN: Is she a coworker?

BARBARA: No.

KEN: Just a friend, then?

BARBARA: No. Actually, this is a little embarrassing — she's my stalker. Sorry. So, you probably read the story in the *Times* about . . .

KEN: I'm sorry, what?

BARBARA: (*Teasing.*) Certainly you've heard of *The New York Times!*

KEN: No, the other part.

BARBARA: Oh. Yes, Lisa stalks me. It's not really a big deal. I'd rather talk about something more interesting.

KEN: I'm sorry . . . I'm a little confused. Do you mean she's in love with you?

BARBARA: Oh — no, no, no. She just emulates me. Have you seen the movie *Single White Female?* It's more that kind of thing. But don't worry — Lisa is completely harmless.

KEN: Oh, I get it. You're a crafty woman, Barbara. That's a good joke.

BARBARA: I'm sorry to say it's not. I really do have a stalker!

KEN: Have you contacted the police? This woman could hurt you! Last year, I had a client who was stalked and she . . .

BARBARA: Lisa, Lisa, Lisa. I don't want to spend our date talking about Lisa!

I'm fine. Let's talk about you. I want to know all about the wonderful world of Ken. How did you spend your day?

(Lisa continues to gaze lovingly at Barbara, copying her movements.)

KEN: OK. Well, there's not really that much to tell. Basically, this morning I got up and . . . I'm sorry, I just get the feeling she's listening to us.

BARBARA: Oh, better than that. She's probably recording us.

KEN: Recording us?

BARBARA: Sure. Oh, it's innocent enough — she'll just go home later and play my voice over and over again. You know how it is. Don't worry, she's not even really listening to you. But she might . . . no, I don't think she has the camera today. But she is wearing my shoes again.

KEN: You let her borrow your shoes?

BARBARA: No, of course not. That would be foolish, wouldn't it? But she does break into my apartment from time to time. I used to change the locks, but that got expensive. Sure, she takes things . . .

KEN: She steals from you?

BARBARA: She always gives them back. And she takes really good care of them. Once, she borrowed one of my suits, and it came back in a dry-cleaner's bag!

KEN: She has your suits dry-cleaned. You seem awfully cavalier about this, Barbara. What exactly are her intentions? Don't you think this is a little dangerous?

BARBARA: Let's forget about Lisa for now, huh? Trust me, I can handle my own stalker. I've been doing so for quite some time, thank you very much. Now, you told me last week that you love skiing. What else do you like to do for fun?

KEN: Uh, let's see . . . I got into biking a couple of years ago. It's a great way to relieve stress.

BARBARA: Big-shot lawyers have a lot of stress, I presume.

KEN: Well, yes. I like to read, but I must admit that I watch more TV than I should. People think lawyers don't watch *Law and Order*, but I love it.

BARBARA: Me too! We have so much in common. What do you like to read?

(Lisa moves closer.)

KEN: It may be cheesy, but I love a good John Grisham novel . . . I'm sorry, is she moving this way?

BARBARA: Who?

KEN: Your little friend.

BARBARA: You mean Lisa? She's hardly my friend. Clearly you've never had a stalker. No, she's more like a petulant sibling, or an extra limb.

KEN: Well, your extra limb is getting closer.

BARBARA: Oh, yep. Looks like it.

KEN: How do we get your extra limb to move further away?

BARBARA: I don't know, really. Usually ignoring her works.

KEN: Listen, Barbara. I really like you and we had a great first date. But I find being watched a little unnerving. Couldn't we just go get a drink somewhere else?

BARBARA: We could, but she'd follow us. She is a stalker, after all.

KEN: Could we just ask her to go away?

BARBARA: We could, but she'd cry. And trust me, her cry is hideous. Have you ever heard a goat being tortured? It's worse.

KEN: Have you heard a goat being tortured?

BARBARA: Well, I can imagine.

KEN: Maybe if we change seats, I could ignore her better.

BARBARA: What?

KEN: Lisa.

BARBARA: Sorry, I was still thinking about the goat. Yes, good idea.
(They switch seats.)

KEN: Aaah, this is better. I can hardly see her at all now.

BARBARA: Good. Now, do you believe in astrology? And I'm only asking because I had this very strange experience once. I was with this guy and . . . what? What's wrong now?

KEN: I'm sorry, it's just that she moved again.

BARBARA: Sorry — I forgot how she loves to see me in profile. I think her Web site says something about the shape of my nose . . . it's so silly . . .

KEN: She has a Web site. OK . . .

BARBARA: Oh, it's just a little thing, really. Just seven or eight pages of pictures of me. Some of them are of me as a child. I'm not quite sure how she got those. And would you believe that there are over a hundred sonnets written in my honor? She's actually quite a good poet.

KEN: You know, I'm beginning to think you enjoy all of this.

BARBARA: Well, sonnets are better than, say, limericks — don't you think?

KEN: Sure. You know what? I'm not sure things are going to work out between the three of us. In fact, I'd recommend that you file a restraining order against this young woman before anything more serious happens.

BARBARA: Oh, please don't leave because of Lisa. I convinced her not to show up on the first dates, but I can't tell you how many second dates she's ruined for me. I feel sorry for her, following a lousy lounge singer all around the city.

KEN: You're not a lousy singer. I'm sure you're a great singer.

BARBARA: I guess I get a small thrill out of her interest in me. I know she'll move on to some other two-bit performer any day now. I just want to appreciate her attention while she's still around. Is that so horrible?

KEN: No, I guess not. She is kind of cute, I guess.

BARBARA: See? Just like a sweet little pet. Now it's not so bad, is it?

KEN: I guess not. Hell, let's invite her for a drink with us.

BARBARA: I don't think that's necessary.

KEN: Lisa! Come over here for a minute!

(Lisa approaches the table.)

Aren't you going to introduce us?

BARBARA: Ken, this is Lisa. Lisa, Ken.

(Lisa waves.)

KEN: Hi, Lisa. Pleased to meet you.

BARBARA: *(To Lisa.)* Isn't he the most handsome one I've been out with all month?

(Lisa nods enthusiastically.)

BARBARA: *(Continued.)* Now, Lisa, you may record anything you wish. But you may not take pictures of this nice man, OK?

(To Ken.)

Next thing you know, there would be a virtual voodoo doll of you on the Web page.

(To Lisa.)

Now, Ken and I are going to talk. You just be still and quiet, OK?

KEN: I don't mind if she talks.

BARBARA: *(To Ken.)* I can take care of my own stalker, thank you.

(To Lisa.)

Still and quiet, Lisa. Not seen or heard.

(Lisa nods.)

KEN: Do you speak?

(Lisa nods.)

BARBARA: I know I'm asking a lot of you, Ken. But could you just try to pretend she's not here?

(Lisa sulks.)

BARBARA: *(Continued.)* I'm sorry, darling, but it is hard to talk about certain things when you're around. Come now, you know I wouldn't want to be stalked by anyone but you.

(Lisa brightens.)

Good girl. Such a good little stalker.

KEN: OK — all right. This is seriously not going to work out. Usually I try to keep my personal and professional lives separate, but it feels vaguely criminal to watch you treat this woman like a pet monkey. And what she's doing to you is at least a Class B misdemeanor in the State of New York. So if you need legal help, please give me a call. Here's my card. I hope that's not too presumptuous. And I'm sorry, but I don't want to go on another date with the two of you.

BARBARA: Well, maybe I'll stay home next time so you can have Lisa all to yourself! Is that what you want?

KEN: What are you talking about?

BARBARA: I saw you looking at her from the moment we entered this restaurant! Making eyes!

KEN: She was leering at you!

BARBARA: Lisa does not leer! She gazes — and with great respect, I might add.

KEN: It was lovely meeting you, Barbara, but I have to go now.

BARBARA: Fine! And you know why that doesn't bother me? Because I already have someone who cares about me! I have someone to listen to my problems, and be interested in my daily life, and take hundreds of pictures of me! I exist, Ken! I affect people! There is a wonderful woman who spends her every waking moment thinking about the presents she will leave me the next time she breaks into my apartment! Think someone will ever be that obsessed with you, Ken? I doubt it — and Lisa doubts it, too!

KEN: (*Pause.*) Well then. May you two live happily ever after.
 (*He exits.*)

BARBARA: Hmph. Just like all the rest.

LISA: He's gone.

BARBARA: And good riddance to bad rubbish. Right, Lisa? What do you say we have a beer and talk about what a good singer I am.

LISA: I miss him.
 (*She exits.*)

BARBARA: Lisa? LISA!
 (*Curtain.*)

END OF PLAY

Who's on Faust?

MARK SAUNDERS

CHARACTERS

REVEREND BILLY RAE GOODSON: male TV preacher with the classic thick hair

BEELZIE: female, dressed in black, no-nonsense type

JONATHAN FAUST: male, young and innocent by all appearances

SETTING

Interior, contemporary church

TIME

Daytime

．　　．　　．

At Rise. The reverend holds a bible in one hand and a sheet of paper in his other. He exaggerates his actions as he prances and struts, rolls his eyes, dips and shakes and waves his fist in the air. He's the only one in the church.

GOODSON: I'm talking about the little things, people. The small things. Itsy-bitsy microscopic things. What most people don't notice. You think the devil's the only one interested in details? Think again. Because my friends, it's not the great fires of London. The great wars of Europe. The great earthquakes of San Francisco we need fear most. No, ma-am. No, sir. It's the little things that count, that make the difference. Separate us from slime and barn animals, separate us from evil. I say the little things. *(Pause.)*

GOODSON: Like shaving. It's a simple truth. If a man cannot shave his face daily, then how can he lead a virtuous life? It's just not possible, friends. Ain't gonna happen. Not in my lifetime. Not in your lifetime. Not in his lifetime. And you know why? Cause it's a little thing. And even the biggest thing is made up of a bunch of little things. You've heard the expression, "Good things come in small packages?" Well, small things lead to good things. That's all I'm saying.

(A business woman in a dark suit enters and slowly walks toward the reverend. It's Beelzie.)

(Pause.)

GOODSON: Oh, sure. The apostles didn't shave. But let's not forget Judas. Do I hear an Amen?

(The reverend stops and looks at his notes, unaware of Beelzie's presence.)

GOODSON: But let's not forget Judas. Judas. I said Judas. Do I hear an Amen?

(Pause.)

GOODSON: Now some of you are sitting there scratching your heads, looking sort of confused, and saying, yeah, but didn't Jesus wear a beard? Jesus. Might I remind you. *JESUS* was the Son of God. Are you the Son of God? Can you transform water into wine? Heal the sick? Raise the dead? Redeem my sins? Yes, people. It's all about sin. Not shaving can lead to sinning. Amen.

(Pause.)

GOODSON: Shame on the unshaven. Shame. Shame. You're telling me, Jesus died for your sins and you can't even spend one minute with a razor in the morning? A clear face is an honest face, and an honest face is a tribute to the great Lord all mighty. Praise be. So, when you go home today, look in your mirror and check yourself out carefully. Ask yourself, am I clean? And if you are not clean, then take out that razor and do the right thing. It's a small step but a step in the right direction. And we all know where the other direction ends —

(Beelzie claps loudly.)

BEELZIE: Ah, yes, I so love the details.

(Goodson jumps.)

GOODSON: What are you doing here, Beelzie?

BEELZIE: You need to ask?

GOODSON: I don't?

BEELZIE: We have a problem. Or, I should say *you* have a problem.

GOODSON: Oh?

BEELZIE: You're behind in your quota.

GOODSON: Nonsense.

BEELZIE: You're sending us bogus prospects, Billy Rae. Useless crapola. Wishy-washy customers at best. Some hardly worth the effort. Most not worth saving, let alone damning.

GOODSON: I don't see how —

BEELZIE: Sin's everywhere. Porn on the Web. Gangsta rap on the radio. Huck Finn in the library. Bars open on Sundays. Why, every Indian tribe in America has its own casino.

GOODSON: That's not good???

BEELZIE: What's not good is, nobody cares. We're in the sin business and nobody cares. We've become a bloody commodity.

GOODSON: Come again.

BEELZIE: They don't believe what they're doing is a sin.

GOODSON: You've been very successful.

BEELZIE: Don't try to brown-nose me. I can't do my job unless you first put the fear of eternal fire into their sinful heads . . .

GOODSON: I fail to see —

BEELZIE: — The idiots look forward to damnation, the few that still believe it, like it's some kind of tropical vacation.

GOODSON: I never agreed to —

BEELZIE: — I'm not happy. But you have bigger problems. My boss is not happy. Now *that's* a problem.

GOODSON: Not happy?

BEELZIE: And you know what that means?

GOODSON: I can guess.

BEELZIE: I'm here to collect your soul.

(Goodson drops to his knees and begins begging.)

GOODSON: Oh, no. Mother of Mercy. No. No. No. No. Please. You can't do this. We had an agreement. Spare me. Oh, spare me. I'm not ready. My show's been extended. I just refinanced the church, under 6 percent. And I'm working on a sermon right now that's a real attention grabber.

BEELZIE: The sin of facial hair? Give me a break.

(Goodson stands.)

GOODSON: But why me? Why? I'm a miserable son of a bitch.

BEELZIE: Miserable, yes, but you still believe.

GOODSON: Now's not a good time.

BEELZIE: It never is, is it?

GOODSON: Look. My soul's pathetic. How about I get you a better soul? The next person, who walks in that door, is yours. I'll do what I can to make it happen. I promise. My mother's due any minute. She's a good woman. Hardworking. Decent. A good soul if ever there was one.

BEELZIE: The next person?

(Jonthan Faust, a fresh-faced teenager, enters the church at the far end.)

GOODSON: I promise. I'll get you a beautiful, untarnished soul. A soul you'd be proud to hang in your office. A magnanimous soul. A soul that —

FAUST: Excuse me? Hello? I was wondering if you could help.

GOODSON: What?

FAUST: I'm lost and saw this church. I thought, you know, you might point me in the right direction.

(Goodson and Beelzie walk toward the young man, who walks toward them. All stop walking when they get close enough to reach out and touch each other.)

GOODSON: How old are you, son?

FAUST: Eighteen.

GOODSON: From around here?

FAUST: No.

GOODSON: *(Aside to Beelzie.)* And as pure as the driven snow, by the looks of it.

FAUST: What?

GOODSON: Welcome. Welcome. Welcome. What brings you here?

FAUST: A bus. I must have got off at the wrong stop.

GOODSON: Bingo!

FAUST: Nope. Not Bingo. Here for the baseball card show at the coliseum.

BEELZIE: Perhaps I can help.

FAUST: *(Addressing Beelzie.)* You a collector?

BEELZIE: You could say that. How'd you like to have the best baseball card collection ever assembled?

FAUST: Yeah, right.

BEELZIE: It's yours if you want it.

FAUST: That can't be cheap.

BEELZIE: We have a deferred payment plan.

FAUST: Yeah?

(Goodson takes Faust by the arm, then puts his index finger against the side of his own nose.)

GOODSON: Listen to her, my son. She's connected.

FAUST: So, yeah, OK. What do I, like, have to do to get the cards? You're not going to take me in some back room and —

BEELZIE: — No. No. No. Not at all. Nothing like that. Strictly business. I get you the cards and you give me your —

GOODSON: Soul.

FAUST: What?

BEELZIE: When you die, I get your soul. For eternity.

FAUST: You're trying to rip off a kid, aren't you? Don't think I know any better because I got zits. Swap baseball cards for my soul. Yeah, right. What else are you offering?

(Beelzie pulls car keys from her pocket and dangles them in front of the boy.)

BEELZIE: An Aston-Martin in the parking lot.

(Faust grabs the keys.)

FAUST: Is that all?

BEELZIE: Is that all! My you are a spoiled boy, aren't you? Let's see. There's a stacked blonde sitting in the passenger seat — a real hottie — and a winning lottery ticket in the glove compartment. The cards are in the trunk.

FAUST: So, let me see if I understand what we're talking about. I sign over my soul to you and I get to keep the cards, the babe, the wheels?

BEELZIE: And you'll lead a charmed life. Until you die. Then it's my turn.

FAUST: Payback time.

GOODSON: Average life expectancy for an American male is 72.5. That's sixty years of getting whatever you want.

FAUST: More like fifty-five.

GOODSON: I'm an optimist. I always round up.

FAUST: Sulphur. Brimstone. Fire. Forever. All that stuff?

GOODSON: Over-rated.

FAUST: The weeping and gnashing of teeth?

GOODSON: A minor distraction.

(Faust sits and ponders. Beelzie paces, as she chants into the young man's ear.)

BEELZIE: Babe Ruth. Ty Cobb. Connie Mack. Walter Johnson. Shoeless Joe. Cy Young. Christy Matheson. The Yankee Clipper. Jackie Robinson. Warren Spahn. Hank Aaron.

FAUST: A 1910 Honus Wagner?

BEELZIE: The American Tobacco Company version or the Fatima team?

FAUST: The T-206. What condition?

BEELZIE: Mint. Of course. Covered in plastic sleeves.

FAUST: Top loader?

BEELZIE: Only the best. Yours if you sign.

FAUST: You rock, lady. Give me the papers.

(Beelzie removes a legal document from one pocket and a pen from another pocket.)

FAUST: Wait. We need a witness.

GOODSON: I'll witness.

(Faust and Goodson sign. Beelzie grabs and signs contract, reviews it quickly, rolls it up and puts it away. Faust walks up to Beelzie.)

FAUST: Hold out your hands. Close your eyes. *(Pause.)* Come on. I'm not going to hurt you.

(Beelzie does as told. Faust walks over and mimes putting something in her hands.)

FAUST: You can open them.

BEELZIE: You're a weird kid, you know that?

FAUST: Why wait until I die? I just handed you my soul.

(Beelzie looks at her hands.)

BEELZIE: There's nothing there.

FAUST: Of course. I don't believe I have a soul, so that's what I gave you.

BEELZIE: What's that?

FAUST: Nothing. My daddy's a lawyer. Contract law. You can't sell what you don't own. But if you believe there's something there, more power to you, and there's due consideration on both sides.

BEELZIE: What?

FAUST: My daddy never cared too much for sin as a community concept, you know. Sin was more personal. I was raised to believe in the Law.

BEELZIE: The Law?

FAUST: Yes, ma-am. The Law.

BEELZIE: The Law.

GOODSON: The Law. What about sin?

FAUST: Sin is whatever makes me feel bad.

BEELZIE: And the baseball cards?

FAUST: Make me feel great. A deal's a deal. Car's out back, right?

GOODSON: Ohhhhhhhh.

(Faust exits, twirling his car keys. Beelzie, her hands extended palm up, watches. Then, she slowly turns her hands palm down and walks over to Goodson. She places her hands on Goodson's neck and begins squeezing. Goodson drops to the floor.)

GOODSON: Wait. Wait. Give me one more chance. I have an idea. I'll get you one hundred souls next week. One hundred. I promise.

BEELZIE: One hundred?

(Beelzie releases her grip on Goodson.)

GOODSON: Guaranteed.

BEELZIE: You have ten seconds to convince me.

GOODSON: There's a multilevel marketing convention coming to town. You know, network marketers? Vitamins. Cosmetics.

(Beat as they both think about it.)

BEELZIE: Multilevel marketing, huh? That's good. Those guys will *sell any-thing.*

GOODSON: And they *believe* in everything.

(Beelzie and Goodson shake hands and laugh, as lights fade.)

END OF PLAY

Works in Progress

SYLVIA REED

Works in Progress was originally produced by Theatre Odyssey, of Longboat Key, Fla., at The Backlot Theatre, 2208 Industrial Blvd., Sarasota, Fla., on March 2–4, 2007. The play was directed by Jack Eddleman, with Jeffery Kin as artistic director. The cast consisted of: #1 — Shelby Eddleman, #2 — Clair Lockeyear, #3 — Judy Phelan.

CHARACTERS

THREE WOMEN:

#1: a young woman in her teens.

#2: early thirties, she holds a baby, wears a large shirt and pants, fuzzy slippers

#3: late forties, wears a nice dress, perhaps a bit tight in places, high heels

SETTING

A stage

TIME

The present (and the past, which is ever-present)

. . .

Three women: They each stand before an easel. #1's easel holds a poster board (science fair project.); #2's easel holds a painting, a work in progress; #3's easel holds a mirror

#1: *(To the audience.)* I'm very smart. My mom says I should be a doctor. I bought *Gray's Anatomy* at a garage sale the other day.

#3: *(To #1.)* I love that show.

#1: *(To #3.)* It's a book.

#3: *(Remembering.)* Oh, yeah. Right.

#1: But my favorite book is the *Atlas of the Human Body.* Did you know we have a mammary ridge? Sounds like a place where you go hiking. I know a boy who has three nipples.

#2: *(She either rocks or nurses her baby.)* I could use another one.

#1: *(To the audience.)* Most people only develop two nipples at the fourth site of the mammary ridge. The other three sites run down your body toward your legs even. *(To #2.)* He's in my class, the boy with three nipples. He showed it to me last year when we were in middle school. He made me pay him a buck. That's how I got to see it.

#2: *(To #1.)* I just had my baby.

#1: Boy or girl?

#2: Girl.

#1: I always get called to babysit. I make excuses.

#2: Oh.

#1: I'm not sure if I like babies.

#3: *(Turning and smoothing her dress over her stomach, looking at herself.)* I don't know about this dress.

#1: On page 1022 of *Gray's Anatomy* it calls the breasts eminences. Sounds like they're royalty, doesn't it?

#2: They used to be.

#3: *(To herself, looking in the mirror, pushing back her neck as if she's had a "lift.")* What is happening to my neck?
(To the audience.) I'm on the verge of fifty. And my daughter is getting married. I'm practically a grandmother.

#2: I used to be an artist.

#1: *(To #2.)* You aren't anymore?

#3: *(To the audience.)* Don't get me wrong. My daughter isn't pregnant. She doesn't have to get married. Not that anyone really has to these days, but you know what I mean. It's just
(In disbelief.) My daughter is getting married. Before you know it, I'll be a grandmother. When did this happen?

#1: *(To #2.)* So what happened to the art?

#2: *(To #1.)* Don't have the time. But I try to squeeze it in.
(Gesturing to the painting.) This is a work in progress.
(Gesturing toward 1's easel.) And yours?

#1: Science fair project.

#2: There was a time when I loved science too. Medical stuff. Like you.

#1: I'm investigating whether age and gender play a role in short-term memory.

#2: That's pretty fancy.

#1: There are twenty silhouettes pasted to this board. Various things. Like a flower. A football. A high-heeled shoe. A baseball bat. Ten of the items are things I believe a boy would most likely remember. Boy things. Like the baseball bat. And ten of the items are things I believe a girl would most likely remember. Like the high-heeled shoe. So I took it to the elementary school down the street from my house and showed it to a group of kindergarteners. They only had a minute to look at the poster, and then they had to tell me what was on it. The little girls remembered the girlie things more often, and the little boys remembered the boy stuff more easily.

#2: I guess that wasn't a surprise.

#1: No. But when I showed the older kids the poster, it switched. The twelve-year-old boys remembered more girl things and the twelve-year-old girls remembered more boy things.

#2: They started to notice the opposite sex, huh?

#1: That's my conclusion.

#2: Interesting.

#1: I better win first place.

#2: You probably have a shot. You're pretty amazing, you know?

#1: *(Pleased with herself.)* Thank you.

#3: *(To the audience.)* Today I cried in church. It was so embarrassing. I'm sitting there in the pew and we start singing this song and it just overcomes me, the tears, and they start rolling down my cheeks and I'm surreptitiously wiping at my eyes trying not to draw too much attention.

#2: *(To #1.)* I would be so happy . . . I mean . . . thrilled . . . if my daughter turned out like you.

#1: Really?

#2: Funny thing is I didn't think I'd ever have a child. But look at me now.

#1: I made an idiot out of myself at a playground the other day.

#2: You did?

#1: My mom made me go with my little cousins. And they were on this merry-go-round and I was pushing and making it go really fast and they kept telling me to jump on . . . they were screaming it — jump on! jump on! — and I wouldn't. My feet wouldn't jump. It was so embarrassing.

#2: I doubt it was all that bad.

#3: *(To the audience.)* We were singing that song for All Saint's Day. *And one was a doctor and one was a priest, and one was slain by a fierce wild beast.* You may know the song. My daughter — the one who's getting married — was in the children's choir when she was little. And they sang that song. Each child was assigned a part. The choir director decided my daughter would be the doctor, and when they sang, *And one was a doctor,* my daughter was supposed to hold up the sign that said "doctor." She was so disappointed because she wanted to be the one that was slain by the fierce, wild beast. But they gave that role to a boy. So she had been pouting about being the doctor and I was afraid she was going to hold up the sign begrudgingly, you know, but she didn't. She held it high and proud and smiled so big. I thought my heart would burst. And here we were singing it again all these years later, and I thought about my daughter, so far away, and how I'll be going to her wedding later this year. *(Pause.)*

It's like if you looked at us from a million miles away we'd look like the inner workings of a clock — everyone moving in step with their lives in different places and directions, but all really part of the same thing. And it just sort of hit me. The beauty of it.

#1: I don't think I'm going to get married. I know I'm not having a kid. I know too much.

#2: Trust me. You don't know.

#3: *(To #1.)* You don't.

#1: *(Protesting.)* But my mother tells me I'm very smart.

#3: *(To the audience.)* Of course she told me that. She always told me that. I was smart.

#2: She's asleep.
(Looking heavenward.)
Thank you.
(She gently lays her in the basket.)
Maybe I can work on this painting.
(She starts to paint.)
My work in progress.
(More to herself.)
Sometimes I feel like I'm disintegrating.

#3: *(Nodding, urging #2.)* Paint.

#2: *(Just realizing #3 said something of interest.)* What's that?

#3: Keep painting.
(After a bit.) My feet are killing me. And I don't know about this dress. I was thinking about it for my daughter's wedding. But it feels a bit tight, you know? I know I used to be this size. I didn't have time to try it on. I just grabbed it and bought it thinking I'd take it back if it didn't work. *(To #2.)* Your shoes look so comfortable.

#2: My new look. Baggy clothes and fuzzy slippers.

#3: I remember those days.

#2: I'm busy all day and I don't do anything.

#3: *(Indicating the shoes.)* Can I try them on?

#2: OK.
(#2 takes off the slippers. #3 removes her heels and leaves them at her easel. Goes to #2's easel. Puts her feet in the slippers. Sighs.)

#3: *(Now at #2's easel, looking at the painting.)* I remember these.

#2: The slippers?

#3: No. These . . . fits . . . of creative impulse.

#2: You like to paint.

#3: I used to.

#2: You don't anymore?

#3: I guess I never really was aware that I had stopped. Until now.

#1: I will be a doctor.

#3: *(To #1.)* Maybe.

#1: I will.

#3: Oh, to be young again. To know everything.

#1: You sound like my mother.

#3: Because a part of me is your mother.

#2: Really?

#3: And yours.

#2: Mine?

#3: That little girl who's sleeping so sweetly . . . that was you.

#2: *(A bit uneasy.)* I think I'd like my slippers back.

#3: Sure.

> *(She slips them off, #2 puts them back on, #3 goes back to her heels.)*

#2: I'm going to go back to my work in progress. So if you don't mind, I can't really talk right now. I have to take every moment I can get to immerse myself.

#3: I'm well aware.

#2: I'm not you. And I'm not ever going to become you. Because I'm not ever going to stop painting and not even realize it.

#3: *(To #2.)* Thank you.

#2: For what?

#3: You've made me remember.

> *(To #1.)* And you. Thank you as well. Trust me, you will jump on the merry-go-round.
>
> *(Nodding.)*
>
> You will.

#1: *(To the audience.)* Maybe I'll ask my mom if we can go hiking on the mammary ridge this summer. She'll probably nod and say, that sounds like a good idea. She's busy and sometimes she doesn't really listen.

#2: *(Looks down at her baby, then back at her painting.)* This isn't coming to-gether the way I thought it would. In my mind.

#3: *(To the audience.)* It seldom does. But maybe that's what makes it so . . . wondrous.

END OF PLAY

PLAYS FOR
FOUR ACTORS

The Girl's Last Big Mistake

DIANA AMSTERDAM

The Girl's Last Big Mistake was produced on Monday July 3, 2006, at Where Eagles Dare Theatre, New York City. Director, Richard MacDonald; lights, Raynelle Wright. Cast: Kitty — Mariana Newhard, Peter — Billy Lyons, Dan — Drew Hildebrand, Jennifer — Jean Lichty.

CHARACTERS
PETER, twenties
KITTY, twenties
JENNIFER, twenties
DAN, twenties

SETTING
In a young couple's apartment

TIME
Present

·   ·   ·

At Rise: Peter is sitting at his computer. He is reading something and laughing. Builds to sidesplitting belly-laugh. Kitty enters, in a jacket.

KITTY: Wow, something's funny.
PETER: Oh my God, oh, you gotta hahahahahahahaha
(She walks up, reads over his shoulder.)
KITTY: "An Absolute Classic." What is this, is it —
PETER: It's e-mails between this pathetic, this total loser girl and this, you'll see, you reading?
KITTY: This is dated like a year —
PETER: Yeah cause it's been, it's been, around the world like six times. Start here. Read it out loud OK?
KITTY: *(Reads.)* "Original message from Finnerty, Shawn —
PETER: Thank you, Finnerty Shawn!
KITTY: "To: Wan, Charlie; Lessard, Jacob; Tsilimos, Raffian; Avidgor, Frucht —
(She has trouble pronouncing this last.)
PETER: Frucht as in Froot with a kuh in it —
KITTY: "Subject: An Absolute Classic. Hey, y'all. One of my friends was on the original list and forwarded this to me. Start at the bottom. It would be difficult for me to be any more . . .
(A hot bright spot, up on Jennifer.)
JENNIFER: . . . miserable right now. I feel like the worst person ever. First, let me start by saying I am very sorry if I ruined your sheets last night—
(This rekindles Peter's giggling.)

(During the following, Kitty is mainly reading off the computer screen; Peter is reading with her.)

(Find places for Peter to laugh out loud; Kitty does not laugh.)

KITTY: She ruined his —

PETER: Yes! Read read.

JENNIFER: I can't believe I did that and there's no way I would have, if I hadn't been sick. I was sick, Dan. I know it looked like I was drunk and I did have a beer at Stephanie's but that's not why I rang your bell at three in the morning. Something I never told you. I have a tendency to get really bad hives —

PETER: She gets really bad hives! hahahahahahaahahah

JENNIFER: I get them when I'm under stress, and you know how much stress we've been under at work, what with Rudy sabotaging my entire packaging program, and the doctor prescribed antihistamines because sometimes the hives spread to my face and then my whole life has to stop, so I took the antihistamines even though I know I can have a reaction, it's a common reaction for some people when they take antihistamines and drink at the same time. Anyway when I got to Stephanie's, Rudy was there, he was there and you weren't, none of the people from our team and I just felt I had to have a beer if I was going to face him, and I drank one, which was really stupid of me but I just didn't think one beer was going to make me sick. I was standing next to Stephanie's fish tank and suddenly I felt I was going to hurl right onto her goldfish. I could barely walk into the bedroom to get my coat without passing out. I've read how people actually die from this antihistamine-liquor reaction and I felt like, the whole world was going black. When I got down onto the street, I was like, Oh my God I can't get into the subway, and I considered a taxi but I had like three bucks and then I remembered that you live like a block away and I thought, Dan wasn't at the party maybe he's home. I somehow made it to your door and I rang your bell, and it was so great of you to let me come up, and I remember, did you make me tea? and then somehow, I was in your bed. I'm not clear on any of that, I know I remember waking up when the room started to get light, and there was that horrible, horrible, that odor, and you were fast asleep, and there was like a rubber on the floor. Did we do anything? I tried to clean the sheets with a wet towel but that only made it worse and I'm just so incredibly embarrassed and sick today, I can't eat, I can't listen to music, I couldn't crack a smile if you paid me and I just feel so stupid. Please don't tell anyone what happened, Dan —

(Lights up on Dan listening.)

JENNIFER: *(Continued.)* . . . it is so humiliating and I know you wouldn't want to humiliate me any further because as it is I feel like I'm not that well liked at work, and you've been my defender and now I think I may have antagonized you too, so whatever happened last night, can we please let it be our secret and please not let it go any further than just the two of us? If you want me to buy you new sheets, I'll be really happy to do that, and you can tell me the exact kind you want because I know you have really good and expensive taste, and I'll get them for you right away. I am so sorry. Jennifer.

PETER: *(Points to computer screen.)* And here's his reply.

DAN: Dear Jennifer. Thank you for your kind apology. I'm sure to file it away under B for Bullshit Long-Winded Rationalization for the Grossest Night of my Life or maybe just under S for Shit. You feel stupid, huh? No. Doing long division and forgetting to carry the one is stupid. Mixing in a red sock with a load of whites is stupid. Staggering into my home at three in the morning, puking with snot running out of your nose, ripping off your clothes and chasing me around the bedroom like a heat-seeking missile and then the clincher, curling up in my bed and doing something that most of us do sitting on an oval seat reading the paper, is not so much stupid as grounds for permanent removal to a psycho ward. Did we do anything? If you mean anything like: touch, trust me, even when you're sober, which you rarely are, I wouldn't touch you with a ten-foot vacuum cleaner, especially now that I've been forced to witness the sight of you in thongs. Have you invested in Vaseline? That would be a good move because you must use gallons to keep your thighs from chafing and oh, about the condom, yes, you did bring several forms of birth control, and while you jumped up and down on my bed, spewing snot and singing "The Dancing Queen," you did toss condoms and your diaphragm, causing me today to disinfect not only the bed but the entire room and trust me, Febreze won't do the trick. And speaking of Clorox, I would like you to replace not only my sheets but my entire bedroom, my apartment and any part of my brain that might remember that sickening stench that rose to my nostrils this morning when I awoke to find you gone, and your corn-dogs still here. That's all I have time to write I'm afraid, I'm off to Central Park to play Frisbee with your diaphragm. Why don't you stop by? All the lads from the office will be there. Dan. P.S. I BCC'd about one hundred people on this, including Rudy and Stephanie and everyone at work. So instead of going into the office tomorrow, why not find the nearest chapter of Alcoholics Anonymous.

(As lights fade on Dan and Jennifer.)

PETER: Do you believe that? Is that the funniest thing you've ever seen?

KITTY: *(After a beat.)* Not really.

PETER: You don't think it's funny?

KITTY: No I don't think it's funny.

PETER: But it's so funny.

KITTY: Not to me.

PETER: C'mon, millions of people have read this, and they all think it's funny —

KITTY: That's what's so horrible, that millions of people have read this.

PETER: And trust me, they all think it's funny —

KITTY: Please don't say "trust me," you know I hate that —

PETER: Believe me, hear me: millions.

KITTY: I don't.

PETER: C'mon, this part where she says, "and there was that horrible, horrible, that smell" — that *smell!*

(Peter breaks into laughter anew. He stops it when he sees how upset Kitty looks.)

PETER: Don't you get what it was?

KITTY: Yes I get what it was.

PETER: And you don't think that's funny? C'mon, how'd he say it — " . . . doing something that most of us do sitting on an oval seat reading the paper," OK that's not the funniest, "while you jumped up and down on my bed, spewing snot and singing 'The Dancing Queen' . . ." Can you picture that?

(Sings.)

You are the Dancing Queen, young and sweet, only seventeen, da-da da-da da-da, Dancing Queen, something something in your tambourine Oh yeah . . . . . .

KITTY: Stop! Just stop! Stop!

(Peter stops singing.)

PETER: Aright, look, why don't you, take off your coat and make yourself a-home, OK? C'mon Kitty you still have your coat on.

(Kitty takes off her coat. There is a long silence between them.)

KITTY: I can't believe you'd laugh at that.

PETER: OK are we still on that, let's get off that OK —

KITTY: I can't believe you'd laugh at that person's pain.

PETER: What do you want for dinner, I'll cook. How 'bout something really unusual like: spaghetti and meat —

KITTY: She probably killed herself.

PETER: No.

KITTY: She writes this guy to apologize and he writes her back this e-mail which is cruel to the point of being sadistic —

PETER: In your opinion.

KITTY: Oh why, is there someone else here?

PETER: What?

KITTY: You always do that, "in your opinion," well if I'm saying it.

PETER: OK y'know what, you want to have a fight, I don't want to have a fight, I want to cook some dinner for both of us —

KITTY: I'm Jennifer.

PETER: What?

KITTY: I'm Jennifer.

PETER: What?

KITTY: I'm Jennifer.

PETER: Your name is Katherine.

KITTY: My name is Katherine Jennifer. Don't you remember, I used to work in packaging?

PETER: That's not possible.

KITTY: I know it isn't. And yet: it's true.

PETER: But you didn't even react when you —

KITTY: When I walked in and saw I couldn't believe it, I thought that thing was dead. But it isn't, it's still inflaming little boys around the world to fits of uncontrollable giggling. This is me, Peter, this is my e-mail, I changed my name afterward that's how bad it got. I thought I could move past this one stupid mistake but it kept following me, and then about a year ago, I. I swallowed forty-eight Advils. I tried to kill myself, Peter —

PETER: No. No. That can't be true. That can't be. There's —

KITTY: Yes yes, I tried to kill myself, because it isn't funny.

PETER: *(Continued.)* . . . no way this could be you, we've been together for six and a half months and this e-mail, it's —

KITTY: Old. Like you said: it's been around the world.

(A long silence, as all this sinks in.)

PETER: So. Why did you just tell me that?

KITTY: Because I think you should know.

PETER: Why did you just make that up?

KITTY: I didn't.

PETER: Yes, you did. I know you did. Because I wrote this.

KITTY: You — you didn't write —

PETER: I wrote this in my writing class, Franco gave an assignment to write a two-character exchange where each character speaks a monologue.

KITTY: No he didn't —

PETER: Kitty! Do you want to see my notes?

KITTY: But why would you write something like that, I don't believe you would, you're not mean and cruel —

PETER: I got the idea from an actual e-mail that went around the world that I read over at Campbell's and I thought hey, that's got monologues, I'll do something like that.

KITTY: Oh.

PETER: Yes. And by the way, I can be mean and cruel.

KITTY: Not with me.

PETER: No not with you because you are . . . someone I love.
(Kitty reacts. The characters Jennifer and Dan come, and pull up chairs or otherwise position themselves like Kitty and Peter.)

PETER: So, why did you make that up, about you being Jennifer? I mean I know you're an actor but, isn't it a bit much to lie to me like that?

KITTY: I don't know.

PETER: You don't know why you lied or you don't know it's a bit —

KITTY: I lied to you because, I was going to tell you the truth but I just wanted to see, would it make any difference if this was me? Because sometimes when something is abstract, when the person who's suffering is unseen and far away, it's easy not to care if they're in pain.
(Beat.)

PETER: Oh.

KITTY: And why did you lie to me?

PETER: Huh? How did I —

KITTY: You told me this has been around the world.

PETER: I wanted a true reaction.

KITTY: Well you got it.

PETER: *(Tenderly.)* Yes. I did.

KITTY: Peter.

PETER: What?

KITTY: That's not the only reason I lied.

PETER: Oh. OK.

KITTY: One time I.

PETER: One time you.

KITTY: One time I stood on a bar in a crowded restaurant, and sang "The Dancing Queen." I stripped down to my bra and panties and threw my clothes into the crowd. I fell off the bar and puked right in some guy's shoe.

PETER: That doesn't sound so bad.

KITTY: He was my boss.

(Peter laughs a little. Kitty laughs a little.)

(Jennifer and Dan laugh, too.)

PETER: So. While we're on the big truth serum. Did you ever actually, try to kill yourself.

KITTY: No.

(Beat.)

KITTY: Y'know, your writing is pretty good.

PETER: Yeah? You think I should try to get it published? Or pretend it's real and send it out like it really happened —

KITTY: No!

PETER: Why not?

KITTY: It's not a joke, it's not funny!

PETER: I'll look at it again.

(Lights down.)

END OF PLAY

Kickass Librarian

JASON WILKINS

Kickass Librarian was originally performed May 21, 2006, at the Boston Theater Marathon, Calderwood Pavilion, Boston Center for the Arts. It was performed and produced by members of The Escapists, with the following cast: Ariel — Ariel Francoeur, Brian — Keith Anctil, Sheila — Cathy Counts, Agent — Chris Fitze. Directed by R. J. McComish.

CHARACTERS

ARIEL: a young librarian with glasses, a neat dark outfit, perfect poise
BRIAN: a shy and smitten young man, nervous
SHEILA: a slightly older woman, careless in her reading habits
AGENT: a slightly impatient but rigidly formal black-suited fellow

SETTING

A typical small-city library

• • •

Ariel, wearing just a hint of leather and sitting up straight as a ramrod, is working the front desk, where she has a phone and a computer. She is the picture of efficiency. Brian is working at a computer station nearby, and he keeps sneaking nervous looks at Ariel. The phone rings.

ARIEL: Front desk, how may I help you? The library is open Monday through Friday from ten to five. You're welcome.
(Phone rings.)
ARIEL: Front desk, how may I help you? Yes, the capitol of Nevada is Carson City. You're welcome.
(Brian sheepishly approaches Ariel.)
BRIAN: Excuse me, ma'am?
ARIEL: Miss.
BRIAN: Sorry?
ARIEL: According to Emily Post, it is most proper for a young man to address a young woman as "Miss," not "Ma'am," since the latter form of address has an unflattering whiff of spinsterhood about it. May I help you?
BRIAN: Uh, I was wondering if you could just turn off the Internet filter on computer station number three.
ARIEL: All righty. *(Clickity-clack on the keyboard.)* Done.
BRIAN: I'm not going to look at porn or anything.
ARIEL: All righty. *(He slinks away; phone rings.)* Front desk, how may I help you? Yes? Well, quantum mechanics *are* compatible with classical mechanics in physical situations where classical mechanics agree with experiment . . . you're welcome.
(Enter Sheila, carrying a battered paperback.)
SHEILA: I need to return this. I think it's a little late.
ARIEL: All righty . . . actually, this book is *very* late. Six weeks late.

SHEILA: Sorry, I've been traveling. What do I owe?

ARIEL: That's actually a good question. As it happens, there is a waiting list for this book. There are fourteen names on it. One might say that you owe all fourteen of those people an apology.

SHEILA: Well, I —

ARIEL: Then again, maybe they all owe you a word of thanks. After all, you have thus far saved them from the brain-rotting literary Ebola that is *The Da Vinci Code.*

SHEILA: Really? I heard it was good. I never actually got around to reading it, myself.

ARIEL: Ah. So, apparently you see the public library, our temple of shared learning, the repository of thousands of years of intellectual inquiry, the last truly democratic institution in America, as a source of paperweights?

SHEILA: Can I please just pay the fines and —

ARIEL: Is this a COFFEE STAIN? Have you no sense of decency??

SHEILA: Lighten up! It's only a book!

ARIEL: Only a book??? Get out of here before I kick your ass!

SHEILA: What?

ARIEL: Even this mass-market piece of crap has more of a spine than you do! Next time you need an airplane book, go to Borders like the rest of the sheep!

(Sheila flees, tossing dollar bills behind her as she goes. Ariel picks them up.)

BRIAN: Wow, you sure do take your work seriously.

ARIEL: Yes. We librarians are a dedicated lot. Ours is a high calling.

BRIAN: Really?

ARIEL: Oh, yes. If knowledge is power, then I'm in charge of an arsenal.

BRIAN: I never thought of it that way.

ARIEL: See? You just learned something. Doesn't it feel good? You know, every time you learn something new, the very structure of your brain is changed. Little sparks fly across the gaps between cells, and your skull is alive with electric fire. Your brain expands, grows more sensitive, more powerful, more . . . sexy.

BRIAN: Sexy?

ARIEL: Oh, yes. All sensations register in the brain, so sex really is in the head. And the bigger the brain . . . I'm sorry, I got off track there for a moment. May I help you with something?

BRIAN: *(Visibly aroused.)* What? Oh, no, thanks. I'm not looking at porn!

ARIEL: All righty. Why not? *(Phone rings.)* Please excuse me. Front desk, how may I help you? Yes . . . actually, the lyrics to "Louie, Louie" are not at all obscene, although if you listen carefully to the original recording, you can hear the drummer click his sticks together and shout the word "Fuck." Yes, really. You're welcome, Timmy.

(Enter the Agent.)

AGENT: Are you the head librarian?

ARIEL: Yes. How may I help you?

AGENT: I'm Special Agent Ringworm with the Federal Bureau of Investigation. I'm here to inspect some of your records.

ARIEL: I see. Well, government documents are stored in the stacks on the basement level —

AGENT: That's not what I mean, ma'am.

ARIEL: Miss.

AGENT: I have to call you ma'am, ma'am. Regulations. I'm here to look at your —

ARIEL: One moment please. *(Types furiously for a few moments.)* You were saying, Special Agent Ringworm?

AGENT: I was saying, ma'am, that I'm here to look at your circulation records.

ARIEL: Why? Do you think you might have an overdue book?

AGENT: Ma'am, we at the FBI would like to know if any of your patrons are checking out materials of a suspicious nature. Books on chemistry, Arabic language manuals, Michael Moore DVDs — stuff like that.

ARIEL: I see. And I assume you claim the authority to invade the privacy of my patrons under the provisions of the Patriot Act?

(Ariel has popped all those p's, lightly and "accidentally" spitting on the Agent. He slowly wipes his face clean.)

AGENT: Yes, ma'am, that's right.

ARIEL: I see. Well, I'm afraid I can't help you with that, Special Agent Ringworm. I seem to have just deleted all of the circulation records from our system.

AGENT: You what?

ARIEL: Silly me. I'll never get the hang of this darn computer.

AGENT: I could arrest you, ma'am.

ARIEL: For what? Refusing to give you something I don't have?

AGENT: How about this. You tell me if anyone in this library right now has asked you to turn off the Internet filter.

ARIEL: Why do you want to know that?

AGENT: This is a matter of national security, ma'am, and I don't have time for questions from some uppity small-town librarian! Just tell me what I want to know, and I won't have to read you your rights!

ARIEL: I know my rights, Special Agent Ringworm — better than you do, I dare say. Incidentally, have you ever heard of the Song of the Cobra?

AGENT: What's that? A metal band?

ARIEL: No. It is a technique perfected by a sect of Buddhist monks in the highest reaches of the Himalayas. *(She softens her tone of voice.)* They found that if they achieved wisdom, mastered the ways of the orderly mind, and spoke in a gentle, melodic manner reminiscent of the mountain flute, they could easily overpower the weak-minded.

AGENT: The weak-minded?

ARIEL: Yes. Everyone who attempted to drive the monks out of their monastery was eventually found in a puddle of their own drool at the foot of the mountain, babbling like an idiot.

AGENT: Like an idiot?

ARIEL: Yes. Don't you find that fascinating, you crypto-Fascist right-wing storm trooper?

AGENT: Me crypto-Fascist right-wing storm trooper?

ARIEL: Yes, very good. Now why don't you head up to the children's reading room on the second floor? They have free copies of the Bill of Rights for you to read!

AGENT: Bill of Rights for me to read . . . Bill of Rights . . .

(Drooling slightly, the Agent shuffles away.)

BRIAN: That was so cool, what you just did! Thanks for covering for me.

ARIEL: Oh, it's nothing. I'd do the same for any patron. That's the fourth FBI agent we've seen this year.

BRIAN: Cool! Um . . .

ARIEL: May I help you find something?

BRIAN: Well . . . actually, I'm looking for a date.

ARIEL: A date in American history, or —

BRIAN: No, no, not that kind of date, I mean —

ARIEL: Oh! I see.

BRIAN: Yeah! That's why I had you turn off the filter, so I could go to the matchmaker sites and search the Portland area for single women.

ARIEL: Well . . . how's the search going? That is, what search critera have you been using?

BRIAN: So far I've searched by age, zip code, level of education, height, smoker/non-smoker, eye color, Last Good Book Read . . .

ARIEL: *(Visibly aroused.)* My. That's a VERY thorough search. But no luck?

BRIAN: Would you like to go out with me?

ARIEL: Before I answer, I must tell you something that might cause you to think I'm strange.

BRIAN: What is it?

ARIEL: I have tattoos.

BRIAN: You do? Where?

ARIEL: Everywhere. My entire body is an illuminated manuscript. It took me years of patience and pain to achieve it. On this breast I have a little drawing of a nightingale in a tree, and a passage from Keats. On this breast, stars whirl in the night sky. And on my abdomen, well . . .

BRIAN: Oh, I can only imagine!

ARIEL: And on my back there is a detailed map of the Library of Congress.

BRIAN: The Library of Congress!

ARIEL: Oh, it's magnificent. Have you ever seen it?

BRIAN: No, but I hope to get the chance someday!

ARIEL: So — you don't think I'm too strange?

BRIAN: I think you're magnificent!

(They're about to kiss when the phone rings. Ariel snaps immediately back into professional mode.)

ARIEL: The library is open until five. Be here at four fifty-nine. But make sure to take all materials for checkout to the front desk by four-fifty.

BRIAN: Yes, ma'am! *(She raises a finger.)* Miss!

(He exits, she gets the phone.)

ARIEL: Front desk, how may I help you? Yes . . . actually, that's Byron. And the verse goes: "She walks in beauty, like the night / of cloudless climes and starry skies." *(Seems uncertain; peeks for a moment down into her blouse.)* Yes, I'm sure. You're welcome. *(She hangs up, blushes, and smiles.)*

END OF PLAY

Laundromat

NORA CHAU

Laundromat was part of the "Sex and No Sex" readings, which was performed on Saturday November 18, 2006, at Ensemble Studio Theater. The theater company was The Kayak Players. It was produced and directed by Ed Lin. Cast: Martin — Brian Yang, Charlie — Peter Kang, Soraya – Angela Ai, Olive — Cindy Cheung.

CHARACTERS

    MARTIN: a quirky British expatriate who has a hard time communicating with women

    SORAYA: a no-nonsense kind of girl who knows what she likes and despises what she dislikes

    OLIVE: a bubbly flirtatious young women who sees every chance meeting as a possible romance

    CHARLIE: an out-of-work actor who has seen one too many thug movies

SETTING

    A twenty-four-hour laundromat in Jackson Heights, Queens

• • •

ACT I, SCENE 1

Setting: Jackson Heights, Queens. A twenty-four-hour Laundromat. Late night. There's no service attendant in sight. Martin, a British expatriate, walks in with a bag of laundry. The laundromat is empty except for Martin and a lone pretty girl, Soraya, who sits reading a book. Martin starts stuffing the machine with his clothes. He pulls out a questionable shirt and starts to sniff at it. He looks over and sees Soraya right next to him. She's seen the whole thing. He tosses the offending shirt into the machine.

MARTIN: I don't remember wearing that shirt.

SORAYA: Uh huh. Sure it's not some dirty fetish?

MARTIN: Pardon?

    (She just smiles at him before continuing her clothing transfer. He pours the remainder of his clothes into the washing machine.)

SORAYA: You don't separate your colors?

MARTIN: What?

SORAYA: You don't separate your lights from your darks?

MARTIN: I am against segregation of any kind.

SORAYA: It's just laundry.

MARTIN: It's just laundry now but then it progresses to canned goods and then, it's just a hop, skip and jump to humans. Where do we draw the line? We need to be constantly vigilant. It's never just laundry. Is it?

SORAYA: Never mind.

    (Soraya returns to her chair and book. Martin pauses.)

MARTIN: The truth is I only have enough quarters for one load. That's why I don't segregate my clothes.

SORAYA: OK.

MARTIN: *(Mumbling to himself.)* Shit. Brilliant, Martin. *(Martin sits down next to her.)* I usually carry more quarters with me.
(She ignores him.)

MARTIN: I'm not poor. Or cheap. I just don't have enough quarters with me today. I usually do. I think, I bought coffee today with them.

SORAYA: I didn't think you were poor or cheap.

MARTIN: Good. Because I'm not. Poor or cheap.
(She tries to resume her reading.)

MARTIN: *Norwegian Wood.* Murakami. He's one of my favorite authors. I've read all of his books. Well at least the ones translated into English. I really feel a connection with his protagonists. Or at least as much of a connection one can feel since his protagonists' are all essentially loners and lonely and odd. But in a good way. You know what I mean?
(Soraya just nods.)

MARTIN: "April's too lonely a month to spend all alone. In April, everyone around looks happy. People throw their coats off and enjoy each other's company in the sunshine — talking, playing catch, holding hands. But I'm always by myself."

SORAYA: It's June.

MARTIN: It's a quote from *Norwegian Wood.* Maybe you haven't gotten up to it yet. What's your favorite Murakami book?

SORAYA: I don't have one. This is the first book of his I'm reading.

MARTIN: Do you like it? Because I really do.

SORAYA: I like the thirteen pages I've read so far.
(Soraya resumes her reading of the book. He looks over her shoulder and starts to read too.)

MARTIN: Oh, this is a good part. One of my favorite sections in fact —

SORAYA: Do you mind? I — I don't like people reading over my shoulder.

MARTIN: Right. Sorry. I guess, I'll just go sit over there so, you can continue with your reading. Unless you want to talk about the book a little?

SORAYA: No. You sitting over there would be great.
(Martin moves over to the other chairs. Soraya continues reading. After a couple of minutes, Martin moves back over to her.)

MARTIN: Can I just ask you a question? Just one question?

SORAYA: I really —

MARTIN: Please?

SORAYA: OK. If you must.

MARTIN: What exactly did I do to turn you off?

SORAYA: Turn me off? I don't remember being turned on.

MARTIN: I don't mean turned on but I mean there was a minute, a second in the beginning that you were into me. That you thought I was cute. Right? I mean, I didn't imagine that, did I?

SORAYA: No, you didn't.

MARTIN: You were interested in me, right?

SORAYA: Well, I thought you were cute.

MARTIN: Well, then, what was it that turned you off? I just need to know for future reference. I'm trying to improve myself. I've been keeping a list.

SORAYA: Your accent.

MARTIN: What?

SORAYA: Your accent. I have to think too much to understand what you're saying.

MARTIN: You don't understand what I'm saying?

SORAYA: I do but it's a longer process time.

MARTIN: Women usually say my accent is my best feature.

SORAYA: Oh, it is. I just place a big importance on communication and well, I don't deal well with lag time.

MARTIN: Lag time. So, if I didn't have a British accent — you would be interested in me?

SORAYA: Well . . .

MARTIN: Because I've toyed with the idea of taking an accent reduction class. That's how Russell Crowe lost his accent. And well, I guess now is a good time as any to take that class.

SORAYA: You don't need to do that.

MARTIN: Why not? Great. It's not my accent is it? You can be honest with me. I need to know.

SORAYA: Look, I'm just here to do my laundry. Yes, I initially thought it might be fun to pass the time flirting with a cute guy but —

MARTIN: So, it's not my accent. Say it. It's not my accent.

SORAYA: It is.

MARTIN: You said but. But what?

SORAYA: But we don't click. We don't have chemistry.

MARTIN: Oh. How do you know that?

SORAYA: What do you mean?

MARTIN: How do you know we don't have chemistry?

SORAYA: I just do.

MARTIN: But how?

SORAYA: I'm sorry. You're making me uncomfortable. I just want to wait for my laundry and read my book. OK?

MARTIN: Right. Sorry.

(He goes back to the other chairs. She reads. He gets up again and goes to her.)

MARTIN: Chemistry and clicking are two different things, no?

SORAYA: Reading.

MARTIN: Right.

(Martin returns to his chair.)

MARTIN: (First he starts humming the tune then launches into song.)
"I once had a girl,
Or should I say She once had me.
She showed me her room,
Isn't it good?
Norwegian wood.
She asked me to stay and told me sit anywhere,
So I looked around and I noticed there wasn't a chair.
I sat on a rug
Biding my time,
Drinking her wine.
We talked until two,
And then she said —"

SORAYA: Do you mind?

MARTIN: What? You don't like it? It's "Norwegian Wood." They talk about it in your book.

SORAYA: I don't care.

MARTIN: (Mimics her.) I don't care.

SORAYA: What?

MARTIN: Nothing.

(She glares at him before going back to her book.)

MARTIN: It's by The Beatles.

SORAYA: (Not looking up from her book.) I know who it's by. I don't like The Beatles.

MARTIN: Why? Because they're British? You don't like their accents?

SORAYA: Stop talking to me.

MARTIN: Gladly. Hater.

SORAYA: What?

MARTIN: Nothing.

SORAYA: You said something.

MARTIN: Nope. Could you please stop talking to me? I'm waiting for my laundry.

SORAYA: I am not a hater.

MARTIN: Are too. A British hater. Hater of all things from the UK.

SORAYA: I am not talking to you anymore.

MARTIN: Good. And I wasn't talking to you first!

(Olive walks in carrying a large laundry bag. She flashes Martin a big smile. Martin turns away from her.)

MARTIN: Not falling for that.

OLIVE: Excuse me?

MARTIN: What?

OLIVE: Did you say something?

MARTIN: No.

OLIVE: Oh OK. Cause I thought you did.

MARTIN: Are you trying to make conversation with me?

(Olive laughs and begins to unload her laundry into a washing machine. She pulls out panties and bras unabashedly.)

OLIVE: And what if I am?

MARTIN: Why?

OLIVE: What?

MARTIN: Well, let me ask you a question. Do you understand me? Is my accent causing some kind of lag time between what you hear to your brain?

OLIVE: Are you calling me stupid?

MARTIN: No, no. Not at all. I was just told that I'm hard to understand and therefore unsuitable for dating.

OLIVE: Who told you that? Your accent is very sexy.

SORAYA: Oh God.

(Martin and Olive both look at her.)

MARTIN: *(To Soraya.)* She thinks my accent is sexy.

SORAYA: You're not supposed to be talking to me.

MARTIN: *(To Olive.)* We're not talking to each other

OLIVE: Oh. I'm sorry. Are you two dating?

MARTIN: No.

OLIVE: But you're not talking to one another?

MARTIN: She's unfriendly. Unlike you.

(Olive smiles and giggles.)

MARTIN: Do you really think my accent is sexy?

OLIVE: Yes.

MARTIN: I knew it. And how about our chemistry?

OLIVE: We have chemistry?

MARTIN: I mean do we click? Although I would still argue that clicking and chemistry might be two different things.

OLIVE: Don't you feel the chemistry between us right now?

MARTIN: No. I don't know. But I think, you're hot.

OLIVE: Thank you. I think, you're cute but strange.

MARTIN: Bad strange?

OLIVE: No. By the way, I'm a sucker for British accents.

MARTIN: Oh. You mean any ol' person with a British accent could come up to you and say a few words and you'd get hot? Are you not discerning about it?

OLIVE: That's not what I meant.

MARTIN: But you said —

OLIVE: You know what? Never mind.

(She goes to sit by Soraya. He ponders the situation for a few moments before approaching Olive again.)

MARTIN: Did I blow it?

SORAYA: Do you really need to ask that question?

MARTIN: I wasn't talking to you. I was talking to her.

OLIVE: Olive.

MARTIN: Say what now?

OLIVE: My name is Olive.

MARTIN: Oh, I'm Martin.

SORAYA: *(To Olive.)* He's just going to keep talking to you now. You're giving him false hope.

OLIVE: I didn't ask for your opinion.

MARTIN: Ha. Sorry. She just makes my blood boil.

(Soraya turns her back to them.)

MARTIN: So, did I blow it somehow?

OLIVE: Well, you didn't blow it but —

MARTIN: I hate buts. Sorry, continue.

OLIVE: I thought we were talking. Having a good time. Some light flirting. But then you freak out.

MARTIN: I didn't freak out. Or at least I didn't mean to. I think I'm just often misunderstood — maybe it's the accent or I don't know what. I didn't mean to call you easy before — I was just wondering, hoping if maybe there was more to it than my accent.

OLIVE: Well, I don't know you well enough to say what else more there is to it — but remember I told you I thought you're cute.

MARTIN: Oh yes, right. I recall that.

(Olive laughs.)

MARTIN: So what do we do now?

OLIVE: I don't know. Chat. Flirt lightly.

MARTIN: You mean make small talk? I'm not very good at that.

OLIVE: No? Why don't you try it out.

MARTIN: OK, well — you know what perplexes me a lot?

OLIVE: What?

MARTIN: Why do we drive on parkways but park in driveways? I mean is it supposed to be ironic? A careless error some fact checker should have pointed out? A bunch of yes men not daring to disagree? I mean what?

OLIVE: Um, maybe try a different topic of small talk.

MARTIN: You don't like that one?

OLIVE: No.

MARTIN: OK —

SORAYA: This is the stupidest conversation I have ever heard. You two are annoying.

MARTIN: Why are you eavesdropping then?

SORAYA: Eavesdropping?

MARTIN: That's what I said, eavesdropper.

(Charlie enters. He has an empty laundry bag in one hand and a gun in the other.)

CHARLIE: All right you motherfuckers — hands up in the air! This is a hold up, all right? And don't any of you fuck with me today! I'm feeling a little crazy and am not responsible for anything I do!

(Soraya and Olive put their hands up immediately. Martin does not.)

CHARLIE: (To Martin.) You fucking with me?

MARTIN: No.

CHARLIE: Then why aren't your hands up in the air, asshole?

MARTIN: No. I just didn't understand you. You're talking kind of fast.

CHARLIE: Don't fuck with me. I'll blow a hole through your balls.

MARTIN: OK, sorry. There's really no need to curse. There are ladies present.

CHARLIE: Motherfucker, you did not just tell me what to do.

SORAYA: Stop angering him!

CHARLIE: Finally someone who gets the gravity of your predicaments! Now I want all your money and all your jewelry — anything valuable in the bag! All right?

(He tosses the bag to them all. The girls put anything they own of value in. And Martin does the same.)

CHARLIE: All right so who wants to die first?

SORAYA: But we gave you all our money.

CHARLIE: I don't care!

MARTIN: Come on! Let us go.

CHARLIE: Can't do that. I'm feeling a little bloodthirsty today.

MARTIN: OK, let the two of them go — I'll stay.

CHARLIE: Oh, tough guy. I like it. You two can leave. He stays.

OLIVE: I'm not going.

MARTIN: Go. I'll be OK.

CHARLIE: Get the fuck out, girls before I change my mind.

   (Soraya is out the door.)

OLIVE: *(Looks at Martin before leaving.)* Thank you!

CHARLIE: Can I call you if I get out of this alive?

OLIVE: Yes, Olive Kim —

CHARLIE: Get out now.

   (Olive exits. Charlie's gun is still pointed at Martin.)

CHARLIE: You in love with her or something?

MARTIN: No.

CHARLIE: You want her to be your girlfriend.

MARTIN: Do not.

CHARLIE: Liar.

MARTIN: Should we get going? We should, right? They'll probably have called the cops or something. Do you think I should call her?

   (Charlie puts the gun down.)

CHARLIE: Why do you always get to be the hero?

MARTIN: Because you're dating. You have a girlfriend already. Is it call after three days or seven days?

CHARLIE: I don't know.

   (Martin goes to quickly remove his laundry. They're soaking wet.)

MARTIN: You came too soon.

CHARLIE: Don't you ever say that in a sentence to me again asshole.

MARTIN: I never got to put my clothes into the dryer. Tomorrow would be too soon right?

   (He takes underwear out of Olive's washer and puts it into his bag.)

CHARLIE: You're one sick puppy, Martin. One sick puppy.

   (The sound of police sirens in the distance.)

MARTIN: I think, I'll call her later tonight.

END OF PLAY

The Naked People Play

STACEY LANE

The Naked People Play was produced in July 2005 by Run of the Mill Theater in Baltimore, Md., under the direction of Ryan Whinnem. The cast was as follows: Margaret — Diana Cherkas, Jon — Matthew Crosby, Naked Man — Jeremy Blaustein, Naked Woman — Donna Panzer.
The Naked People Play was produced in March 2007 by the Insurrection Theater Company in Phoenix, Ariz., with artistic director Dana Cianciotto. Sarah Turner directed, and the cast was as follows: Margaret — Carrie Benton, Jon — Xchel Hernandez-Zendejas, Naked Man — Shawn Harris, Naked Woman — Veronica Harner.

CHARACTERS
>MARGARET: a clever, self-assured but secretly fragile woman in her mid-
>twenties
>JON: an awkward and high-strung man with good intentions in his mid-
>twenties
>NAKED MAN: a man in his mid-twenties
>NAKED WOMAN: a woman in her mid-twenties

SETTING
>A bare stage with three chairs

TIME
>The present

• • •

Lights come up on a stage containing three simple chairs placed in a row. In the first chair sits a completely Naked Man. In the middle chair, Margaret, fully clothed, sits. In the third chair, a completely Naked Woman sits. Throughout the piece, Margaret looks at the audience and looks at Jon, but never looks at the naked people. From the moment he enters, Jon glues his eyes to the naked people. The Naked Man and the Naked Woman sit completely still, hands strategically placed if need be, and stare forward blankly for the duration of the play.

MARGARET: *(Talking on a cell phone.)* What do you think? He started balling like a little girl. *(Listening.)* Yep. Right in the middle of the restaurant. I only wish I could say I was surprised. *(Listening.)* No, not since —
(There is a knock at the door.)
MARGARET: *(Into phone.)* Hold on. *(Calling as she crosses to the door.)* Who is it?
JON: *(Offstage.)* It's me.
MARGARET: *(Into phone.)* It's him. I got to go. *(Listening.)* OK. Bye. *(Margaret pockets the cell phone and opens the door.)* Hi Jon.
JON: *(Laden with a heart-shaped box of chocolates, red roses, and a teddy bear.)* Margaret, my darling Mar — *(Seeing the naked people and dropping everything in his hands.)* Jiminy Christmas?!
MARGARET: Pardon?
JON: What is going on?
MARGARET: Not much. I was just —

JON: What are you doing, Margaret?

MARGARET: Well, I just was on the phone with —

JON: You're — There are — Are you in trouble? Should I call the police?

MARGARET: No. Jon, I don't know why you're getting so hysterical. There's nothing —

JON: For Pete's sake! You know what I'm talking about.

MARGARET: No, I don't.

JON: *(Pulling her far away from the naked people and whispering.)* There are naked people here!

MARGARET: Oh, right. I forgot about them. Can I get you a Pepsi or something?

JON: You forgot! Margaret, why are there naked people here?

MARGARET: Oh, it doesn't matter.

JON: It doesn't —

MARGARET: So what did you come here to say to me, Jon? Surely you didn't come all this way to discuss the naked people in my living room.

JON: What's wrong with you? There are naked people —

MARGARET: It's my educated guess that you stopped by to try to convince me not to break up with you, so commence convincing. And dear, do hurry, please. This is only a ten-minute play.

JON: Heavens to Betsy! You — you're breaking up with me because you're having a threesome with these naked people!

MARGARET: Don't be silly. I don't even know them.

JON: That's even worse. What kind of sick sexual —

MARGARET: Contrary to popular belief, nudity and sexuality are not synonymous.

JON: What?

MARGARET: Just trust me, dear. It has nothing to do with sex, OK?

JON: What doesn't? Us or the naked people?

MARGARET: Both.

JON: So you aren't dumping me because of the sex —

MARGARET: No.

JON: Oh good. So, um . . . then why is it you're breaking up with me?

MARGARET: I already told you.

JON: You did?

MARGARET: I'm breaking up with you because you don't listen to me.

JON: I do too.

MARGARET: You don't pay attention to me.

JON: I do too.

MARGARET: *(Calmly.)* Your attention span is like that of a — *(Snapping.)* Will you stop looking at the naked people?

JON: Sorry, but its hard not to.

MARGARET: You've seen naked people before, dear.

JON: Not like this. Margaret, what is going on?

MARGARET: Nothing is going on.

JON: *(To the naked people, slowly and loudly.)* Who are you? What are you doing here?

MARGARET: They don't talk.

JON: Please put on your clothing and exit the vicinity immediately.

MARGARET: Why don't you make yourself comfortable. Take off your coat, have a seat —

JON: I am not taking my clothes off.

MARGARET: No one asked you to. Have a seat.

(Margaret leads Jon to the center chair and sits him down.)

JON: Margaret, I am not comfortable with —

MARGARET: Then stop looking at them. Look at me.

JON: Hey, don't get mad at me. *(Pointing to the audience.)* They're doing it too.

MARGARET: I don't see what the big deal is. I know you've seen naked people before and I bet the audience has too. They've been to the movies.

JON: It's different when it's onstage. It's much closer up and more real.

MARGARET: I suppose. Now, Jon dear, let's stop talking about —

JON: Did you invite these naked people to your — Where did you find —

MARGARET: No, don't be silly. They came with the set.

JON: *(Standing.)* This isn't — There's something very wrong going on here.

MARGARET: Being naked is the most natural thing in the world.

JON: Have you become a nudist or something?

MARGARET: Do I look like a nudist to you?

JON: I don't know what a nudist looks like.

MARGARET: Well, they're usually nude, I presume. I'm not.

JON: Are they nudists?

MARGARET: Not to my knowledge.

JON: But they're naked.

MARGARET: Yes, we know. Now, can you try to move past that?

JON: But there are naked people in your —

MARGARET: Yes, I believe you've mentioned that . . . Several times, in fact. Now Jon, I'm sorry, but I really think that we should stop seeing each other.

JON: This is some kinda joke, right? Well, I don't get it.

MARGARET: There's nothing to get. It's not a —

JON: I demand an explanation right now, or I'm leaving!

MARGARET: Like I told you last night, I feel we don't ever really communicate on a deeper —

JON: No. I'm not talking about *us*. I am talking about the naked people.

MARGARET: Really, Jon. It's not a big deal.

JON: Not a big — Why are there —

MARGARET: Isn't it obvious?

JON: No.

MARGARET: Well, if I must spell it out for you . . . It's one of those lofty artistic concepts. You know, symbolism. That naked man represents you —

JON: What?! I'm not naked! I don't know that naked guy. How can he —

MARGARET: And that naked woman represents me.

JON: No, Margaret. What ever you do, do not take your clothes off!

MARGARET: I'm not going to — Will you just shut up and listen to me for once?

JON: I'm listening to you. I always —

MARGARET: They represent our emotional struggle and our fragileness in this crucial breakup scene, because you're never more vulnerable than when you're naked.

JON: That's stupid.

MARGARET: It makes sense. Not an entirely fleshed out idea — no pun intended — but, well it isn't easy to make a statement nowadays when everything's been done before. Plus, nudity helps out with box office sales. *(Winks at audience.)* Now, let's move on with the scene, shall we?

JON: Can't you get them to go away? I am not comfortable with —

MARGARET: Then stop staring at them. I can assure you they aren't going to say anything or do anything to distract you from our dramatic breakup scene. They're just scenery.

JON: How do you know? They might decide to do something. They're naked. They're unpredictable. Just in case, I best keep an eye on them.

MARGARET: Jon, I'm really starting to loose my patience. Focus on me. Is that really that hard for you to do?

JON: Hey, don't blame me. The audience is —

MARGARET: *(Looking out at the audience and speaking to them.)* Will you all please stop staring at the naked people? Watch me. This play is about me. They're just symbols. They don't even have names and I'm the main character. This is absurd. *(To audience.)* You guys are as bad as Jon. *(To Jon.)* I don't think they care if we break up or not. I don't think you care if we break up or not. I don't even know why I'm here. It's over, Jon. Good-bye.

JON: Let's go to a nice restaurant or something and talk this thing out, OK, Margaret? Please.

MARGARET: I am not leaving naked strangers in my apartment!

JON: OK. Then I'll come back later when they're gone and —

MARGARET: Look, Jon, if you want to save this relationship, it's got to be here and now.

JON: But the naked —

MARGARET: Here and now and not another word about the naked people.

JON: But how can I — (*Margaret shoots him a threatening look.*) OK. OK. Fine. (*He moves the center chair downstage, away from the naked people and gestures for Margaret to sit in it. He collects the box of chocolate, teddy bear, and roses and awkwardly hands them to her, clearing his throat.*) Um, I want to stay together, Margaret.

MARGARET: (*Waiting for him to elaborate and realizing he's not going to.*) And?

JON: I don't want you to break up with me.

MARGARET: (*After waiting for him to continue.*) But I just don't think we're connecting anymore.

JON: Of course we are —

MARGARET: Jon, whenever we're together, there's always something else going on in your head and you aren't giving me your full attention.

JON: That's not true!

MARGARET: Jon, this just isn't working.

JON: I know. It's stressful enough having this conversation in front of all these strangers. (*He gestures to the audience.*) But then there's those naked people. Let's go to a nice —

MARGARET: No, I mean us. We don't communicate.

JON: Of course, we communicate. We're communicating right now, aren't we?

MARGARET: No, we aren't. I want your full attention, Jon, and I don't have it. I don't even have half your attention. (*Gesturing to Naked Man.*) He has half of it and (*Gesturing to Naked Woman.*) she has the other.

JON: But it's not normally like this.

MARGARET: It's always like this.

JON: Usually there aren't naked people watching us.

MARGARET: They aren't watching us. They are being watched.

JON: That's not the point.

MARGARET: Yes, it is. Everyone is watching them. No one is watching me. No one is paying attention to me.

JON: I'm paying —

MARGARET: No, you're not.

JON: I'm sorry, Margaret. But it's not my fault. And it's not the audience's fault. There's something about naked people that just catches our attention. It's biological or psychological or something, I don't know. We can't turn away, even if want to. It's like a car wreck.

MARGARET: But that's not right. I am trying to communicate. I am trying to get my message across to you, to *(Gesturing to the audience.)* them. And my message has nothing to do with naked people.

JON: Yeh, that may be true, but if people talk about this play later, they aren't going to talk about your message. They're going to talk about the fact that there were naked people in it.

MARGARET: That's disgusting.

JON: I bet they won't even call it by its name. They'll just call it "The Naked People Play."

MARGARET: They won't even remember our names. Probably not our faces either.

JON: Well, it's probably not the naked people's *faces* they'll be remembering, if that makes you feel any better.

MARGARET: It doesn't. But I guess I get it now.

JON: Get what?

MARGARET: Why they agreed to take off their clothes in front of all these strangers.

JON: Why?

MARGARET: Here we are . . . We're pouring out our hearts and souls up here. And nobody's even going to remember us. They'll just remember the naked people.

JON: Well, they are naked.

MARGARET: Those naked people are stealing our show and they didn't even have to work for it.

JON: Hey, be nice to the naked people. You think it's easy to be naked in front of a bunch of strangers! It isn't even easy being naked in front of people you know. I couldn't do what they're doing.

MARGARET: I could.

JON: No, you couldn't.

MARGARET: If it was for artistic purposes . . .

JON: No, you wouldn't.

MARGARET: Oh yes, I would. To save the show, I would. To make an impact, I would. To be remembered, I would.

JON: No, you wouldn't.

MARGARET: You just watch me! *(Slowly, she begins to unbutton her blouse and then stops. Sadly.)* I . . . I can't do this.

JON: It's OK. You don't have to. Let's go, Margaret. We don't belong here.

MARGARET: But we can't just leave the audience. We're the speaking characters. We're the storyline. We provide the plot. We deliver the catharsis. If we leave now, they'll never find out whether we stay together or break up. They'll be no conclusion. They'll be no lesson. They'll be no point. We can't just leave them like this.

JON: It's what they want. They were never interested in us, anyway.
(Jon exits.)

MARGARET: *(To the audience, darkly, deeply hurt.)* They won't entertain you. They won't enlighten you. They won't challenge you. They won't do anything, but hey! Does that matter? They're naked!
(Margaret storms off. The Naked Man and Naked Woman continue to stare forward, blankly and eerily. An uncomfortable silence lingers. The lights slowly fade to black.)

END OF PLAY

Recognition

WILLIAM BORDEN

Original production at Playwrights' Circle Short Play Festival,
Palm Springs, Calif., January 25–28, 2007. Cast:
Brent — Jim Strait, Alice — Marilee Warner, Susie — Nicole
Pitman, Jonathan — Paul MacKey. Directed by Jim Strait.

CHARACTERS

    BRENT: forty-three
    ALICE: forty-three
    SUSIE: forty-three
    JONATHAN: mid-forties

SETTING

    An upscale restaurant

TIME

    The present

• • •

A restaurant. Brent sits at a table, looking around for someone. He's forty-three, with a nicely trimmed beard. Alice enters, breathless. She's forty-three, wearing something that hearkens back to her days as a hippy. At first they don't recognize each other.

ALICE: Brent?

BRENT: Alice?

ALICE: I would've recognized you anywhere!

BRENT: Me too!

    (They start to hug. They hesitate. They hug. They start to kiss. They hesitate. They brush cheeks. They sit.)

ALICE: Am I late?

BRENT: No, no.

ALICE: I'm always late. Remember? Where's your wife?

BRENT: She's coming. She's shopping. She's usually on time. She's an accountant. Numbers! Where's your husband?

ALICE: Jonathan? He should be here soon. He had a squash game.

BRENT: Squash!

ALICE: Do you play?

BRENT: You know me. No hand-eye coordination. I swim laps. Back and forth. It seems as if you're not going anywhere —

ALICE: You're not.

BRENT: — but it keeps me in shape. It clears my head. It's a kind of meditation. You?

ALICE: Yoga.

BRENT: Really!

ALICE: Soon. When I have time.

BRENT: You look —

ALICE: I've put on weight.

BRENT: I was going to say, you've lost weight.

ALICE: You think so?

BRENT: You look—

ALICE: Your hair's gray. Your beard.

BRENT: Twenty-five years.

ALICE: It seems —

BRENT: Like yesterday!

ALICE: — such a long time ago.

BRENT: That last summer we were together, after we graduated from high school —

ALICE: We were so young! So —

BRENT: — in love . . .

ALICE: — foolish.

BRENT: I remember everything.

ALICE: Do you?

BRENT: This is kind of strange, isn't it?

ALICE: Meeting our spouses?

BRENT: I almost didn't call. But I thought, we're in town for a day . . .

ALICE: I'm glad you called. It's good to see you.

BRENT: I think about you.

ALICE: I think about you, too.

BRENT: Sometimes I wonder what would have happened if we —

(*Susie enters. She's dressed conservatively.*)

SUSIE: There you are!

ALICE: You must be —

BRENT: Susie.

SUSIE: Brent's wife! So nice to meet you!

BRENT: This is —

SUSIE: Alice, of course. He still has your picture.

ALICE: *(To Brent.)* You didn't tell me.

SUSIE: Have you put on a little weight?

BRENT: Actually, she's —

SUSIE: I love your dress! It's so . . . bright!

ALICE: There's Jonathan!

(Jonathan enters. He's clean-shaven, energetic, extraverted.)
Over here!

JONATHAN: *(In great spirits.)* What a game! But I prevailed. You must be
    Brent. And you're Susie. I'm Jonathan. This is great! Have you ordered?
    What a great idea! You two seeing each other again, Susie and I getting
    to meet our old rivals —

SUSIE: Not really rivals . . .

JONATHAN: High school sweethearts — it's a love that never dies. Keep your
    eye on her. She might try to steal him back.

SUSIE: I don't think . . .

ALICE: It's been twenty-five years! I've gotten fat!

SUSIE: Should we order?

JONATHAN: If they get it on, Susie, you and I can —

ALICE: We're only having lunch.

JONATHAN: *(To Alice.)* Remember our first lunch?
    (To the others.) We didn't even wait for dessert. Hotel across the street.
    We were both married. To other people. Spontaneity! That's what I be-
    lieve in. If you feel like doing something, do it! What do you believe in,
    Brent? You're a planner, I'll bet. A thinker. College professor?
    (To Alice.) What did you say? French history?

BRENT: The French revolution.

JONATHAN: Off with their heads! Waiter! Scotch and soda!
    (To Susie.) What'll you have?
    (To unseen waiter.) Make it two!
    (To Alice.) Chablis?
    (To unseen waiter.) Chablis!

SUSIE: I'll have tea.

JONATHAN: Tea! And another for my friend here! What about you two? Sec-
    ond marriage? Third?

BRENT: First for both of us. For me anyway. Maybe Susie hasn't told me about
    the other ones.

SUSIE: We met our freshman year of college. We went steady. We got engaged.
    We graduated. We married. Twenty-one years.

JONATHAN: Good God!
    (To Alice.) How long for us?

ALICE: You know how long we've been married.

JONATHAN: *(To Brent and Susie.)* Twenty-one years! Congratulations! In this day
    and age — one out of every two marriages kaput — how do you do it?

SUSIE: Well, we respect each other.

BRENT: We try to communicate.

SUSIE: We believe in honesty.

BRENT: We have our ups and downs.

SUSIE: Everybody does.

JONATHAN: How many affairs?

SUSIE: I beg your pardon?

ALICE: Don't.

JONATHAN: Twenty-one years of matrimonial bliss, sure, no doubt, but still, the eye wanders, the hormones surge, an enchanted evening, or lunch, a nearby hotel, a business trip out of town — no harm! We're human! Right?

ALICE: I think we should order.

JONATHAN: What was the point of this tête-à-tête, anyway? Wasn't it to see if there was still love juice flowing between the old lovers?
   (To Susie.) What did *you* think the point was?

SUSIE: Old friends . . . Friendship is a valuable thing.

JONATHAN: Friends?

ALICE: *(To Jonathan.)* You said this did not bother you.

JONATHAN: They fucked each other crazy.

BRENT: We don't need to put up with this.

SUSIE: That doesn't matter now.

JONATHAN: If we weren't here, they'd be all over each other.

SUSIE: I trust Brent.

JONATHAN: *(To Alice.)* Did you tell him about Camille?

ALICE: God damn you!

JONATHAN: *(To Brent.)* Your daughter, if I'm not mistaken. She's almost twenty-five. In medical school. Smart! Doesn't like me. Camille. You must have been interested in French history in high school.

BRENT: We met in French class. We spoke French to each other.

SUSIE: *(To Brent.)* You have a daughter?

JONATHAN: Who else's would it be?

BRENT: *(To Alice.)* You never told me.

JONATHAN: Secrets! Secrets!
   (To Susie.) They have secrets.

BRENT: *(To Alice.)* Why didn't you tell me?

JONATHAN: *(To Susie.)* How many children do you have?

ALICE: *(To Brent.)* You went away to college. You wrote me you had met a girl, you had fallen in love.

JONATHAN: How many children?

SUSIE: Three.

JONATHAN: Now four! Alice and I —

(He gestures — none.) But tell us, Brent, if Alice had told you, would you have dropped sweet Susie? Rushed home? Married Alice? Who would Susie have married then? Would Alice and I have had our affair anyway? She would have divorced you, married me? You would have married Susie then?

BRENT: (To Alice.) Where is she?

ALICE: Columbia.

BRENT: You asked me, that summer before I left, when we thought we would get married someday, if we had children, what would we name them. We said —

ALICE: André . . .

BRENT: . . . or Camille.

JONATHAN: Here's her address. Look her up. Surprise her. This was a great idea, this lunch. Old times!

BRENT: (To Alice.) You should have told me.

ALICE: You had found Susie.

JONATHAN: A phone call, no phone call — lives change.

BRENT: You sacrificed everything for me?

ALICE: I didn't sacrifice anything. I raised a wonderful daughter. What would you have done? Left Susie, married me? Out of guilt?

JONATHAN: The future shifts, it buckles, like a bridge in an earthquake.

BRENT: I loved you. I would have loved you.

And thought all this time, what if I had married Susie?

SUSIE: This was a terrible idea.

JONATHAN: (To Brent.) You needed to know.

(To the others.) He needed to know.

SUSIE: No, he didn't!

BRENT: Do you have her picture?

(Alice reaches into her purse.)

JONATHAN: (To Susie.) Do you have pictures of your kids? I'd love to see them.

(Alice hands Brent a photo. Susie exits. Brent looks at the photo. He looks at where Susie has gone.)

Do *you* have pictures of your kids?

(Brent slips the photo into his pocket. He stands. He and Alice look at each other. He exits.)

Waiter!

END OF PLAY

The Third First Blind Double Date

JENNY LYN BADER

The Third First Blind Double Date was first produced in the New Georges Performathon, an all-day marathon of short plays, at Dixon Place in New York City. The play was directed by Julie Kramer. The cast was: Olivia — Jennifer Gibbs, Tom — Ross Gibby, Nancy — Eva Lowe, Adam — Brandon Demery. It received its first run at Henlopen Theatre Project (Artistic Director, Ari Laura Kreith.) in Delaware, directed by Ari Laura Kreith. The cast was: Olivia — Nora Edie, Tom — Michael Lundy, Nancy — Alysia Reiner, Adam — Daniel Talbott. Julie Kramer also directed the 2006 production at NYU/Strasberg, in Jenny Lyn Bader's play cycle *Out of Mind: Seven Short Plays with Some of the People Missing.* The cast was: Olivia — Marna Kohn, Tom — Reese Efle, Nancy — Claire Levin, and Adam — Mardee Bennett.

CHARACTERS

OLIVIA: twenties to thirties, single
TOM: thirties, married
NANCY:, thirties, married
ADAM: twenties to thirties, single

SETTINGS

Scene 1 takes place in a living room, with a table downstage and a couch and chairs upstage. After that, the chairs are moved to the table and the downstage area represents a restaurant.

•   •   •

SCENE 1

A party winding down. Olivia, the last guest, starts to leave. Her friends, the hosts Tom and Nancy, are in high spirits postparty.

OLIVIA: So happy anniversary again. I've had a wonderful evening.

TOM: We're so glad you could make it.

OLIVIA: It's been perfect. Ten years — wow. The only person I've ever known for ten years was a cat. And on that note, I'll let myself out . . . God I can't believe I'm last to leave, that's so tacky!

NANCY: You can stay as long as you want.

OLIVIA: No, I'll just go and leave you to your . . . ten years.

NANCY: We'll leave you to your, what is it now? Six months? I guess Hank couldn't make it tonight? Send him our love!

OLIVIA: Yes, yes! I'll send him your love.
(She pauses and smiles. She puts on her coat. She starts to walk out. Then she changes her mind and turns around.)
Though we broke up.

NANCY AND TOM: What?

OLIVIA: Not to bury the lead or anything. I'm sorry I should've mentioned it earlier it's just that it was your anniversary and . . . Don't worry I'm completely fine with it. And I'm sorry he's not here, he really wanted to come but he couldn't because we broke up yesterday and your party was today. But otherwise he would've been here, he was really excited about it, it's too bad the schedule worked out that way. And also I'm sorry I didn't get you a present, it's just that we broke up yesterday so today has been a big day. *(Beat.)*

NANCY: Are you OK?

OLIVIA: Fine, I'm fine.

TOM: Why don't you sit down.

OLIVIA: I don't want to.

(She sits down.)

NANCY: Have some club soda.

TOM: Have some cashews.

NANCY: Have some whiskey.

OLIVIA: No thanks, I can get drunk on air. And am, I believe.

(She pours herself whiskey.)

I know it's the right thing. It's just, you know, that little pain on the side of my stomach. And a sharp shooting one in my eyebrows?

TOM: I think there's a new aspirin for that.

OLIVIA: There's no aspirin for what I have.

NANCY: He was a sweet guy. Hank.

OLIVIA: He's not dead.

NANCY: I meant, when you were with him, he seemed sweet. Like a sweet soul.

TOM: I never thought you two would end up together.

NANCY: Really? I did.

OLIVIA: You're the only one. I only broke up with him fourteen hours ago and people I thought were my friends are telling me they never liked him anyway and they want to fix me up on blind dates.

NANCY: *(Blurts out.)* Oh I would love to go on a blind date!

TOM: Honey?

OLIVIA: I'm sure she didn't mean that.

NANCY: I did mean it. I love Tom, but it would be so interesting to go out to dinner with someone I don't know or care about at all. I haven't done that in years!

OLIVIA: I think you're better off this way. You're idealizing something unpleasant and occasionally excruciating . . . Remember Greg, the one who turned out to be evil? Or the guy who . . .

TOM: I admit I miss it too. Dating. Not all of it. Just the first date. I miss the first date.

(Silence. Then Nancy is inspired.)

NANCY: Olivia — maybe we could join you!

OLIVIA: Join me?

NANCY: On one of your first dates! When you're up to having one. You know, go double.

OLIVIA: That's ridiculous! A first date is never a double.

TOM: Why not?

OLIVIA: Because a first date means sitting alone with someone you dread who . . .

NANCY: But you just said you didn't like that.

TOM: I think Nancy's plan is a great one. Just as a little anniversary present to us. Let's try it.

(Blackout.)

SCENE 2. THE FIRST "FIRST BLIND DOUBLE DATE"

Lights come up on Nancy and Tom sitting at a table, seated across from Olivia and an empty chair.

NANCY: *(Excited.)* So that must be Matt.

OLIVIA: Where?

NANCY: Right there. He's walking in.

OLIVIA: *(Looking around.)* I don't see him.

(Tom and Nancy watch as the date enters. Tom and Nancy can see him, but Olivia and the audience can't. Tom gets up to make introductions.)

TOM: Matt, I'm Tom, this is Nancy, and *this* is Olivia.

(Olivia looks where "Matt" is supposed to be.)

OLIVIA: Nice to meet you.

TOM: *(To "Matt.")* Oh, the coat check's over there.

OLIVIA: *(Whispers to Nancy, alarmed.)* I still can't see him!

NANCY: Really!

OLIVIA: I mean, he's invisible.

NANCY: Oh he's not that bad!

(Tom and "Matt" sit at the table and sit. Tom addresses the empty chair.)

TOM: So Matt, I assume Sally warned you that Nancy and I would be coming on your date?

(A pause as they listen.)

NANCY: *(Laughing at Matt's response.)* I feel that way too. I mean, I come from a family of five siblings so of course *I* think it's merrier!

TOM: How do you know Sally?

(A beat as they listen. Only Tom and Nancy can hear him.)

NANCY: And do you like working there? Is it true you have the best emergency room in the city?

TOM: *(Laughs.)* Oh that's good. That's very good. "Only if you're already dead!"

(Turns to an ashen Olivia.)

A little doctor humor, that's all.

NANCY: What kind of doctor are you?

(Beat.)

TOM: So you break hearts for a living!

(He laughs again.)

NANCY: Tom. Contain yourself.

TOM: Seriously. That's a lot of pressure. I always say I went into radiology for the schedule but really I can't imagine slicing people open. So what do you think about that monkey-to-human transplant out in California? Did you read about it in yesterday's paper?

("Matt" gives his opinion.)

NANCY: Really? I'm sure the reporter would have noticed if it was a baboon.

("Matt" speaks again as Nancy listens, annoyed.)

Well, it was in *The New York Times!* So of course I assumed it was true!

("Matt" speaks again as Nancy stares and listens.)

You don't have to get so upset about it!

TOM: Honey. Calm down. *(To "Matt.")* What? The men's room? Is that way.

(Tom and Nancy watch him walk away.)

TOM: What do you think?

NANCY: He's smart and funny. But a little bit arrogant and opinionated. Even for a surgeon.

TOM: Maybe you were just a little defensive sweetie. About the *Times.*

NANCY: Of course not sweetie, I'm completely objective about that. What matters is if Olivia likes him.

OLIVIA: Um. I don't know. I can't . . . see him.

NANCY: Yeah. I know. It's hard to visualize it.

OLIVIA: No, but I can't *see* him.

NANCY: *(Concerned.)* What do you mean?

(Lights down.)

SCENE 3. THE SECOND "FIRST BLIND DOUBLE DATE"

NANCY: *(Getting up from the table.)* Hi, you must be Gerald!

OLIVIA: *(Looking in the wrong direction.)* Hi.

NANCY: *(Whispers.)* He's over there. Can't you see this one either??

OLIVIA: No!

TOM: Gerald. Nice to meet you. I'm Tom Durst and this is my wife Nancy. And this is Olivia.

("Gerald" makes a flattering comment to Olivia.)

NANCY: Oh isn't that sweet.

TOM: Of course everyone says that when they first meet Olivia. Not that we've been on many dates with her . . .

NANCY: Actually I've *never* seen a photo that did justice to Olivia. *(Beat.)* What? Oh well she and I were at the *Wall Street Journal* together. She used to do newspaper work before she got into TV reporting. Yeah, and now I work at the *New York Times*. I'm an editor. The travel section.

(Tom listens to the next question.)

TOM: College, actually. Yeah, we're one of *those*. At a party.

NANCY: It wasn't exactly at a party. It was in the library.

TOM: Well, we were in a few of the same lecture classes . . . Remember Percy Harrison? I never listened to a word that man said but he was a great teacher, I thought. We had his class together. And we studied in the same part of the library?

NANCY: We *met* in the library.

TOM: But the first time I really saw her was at the party. You know how you can meet someone, then *really* meet them?

NANCY: We *met* in the library.

TOM: But I mean really meet. Really — kaboom, you know?

OLIVIA: No. I don't.

TOM: Gerald. You've gotten us talking about ourselves just when we're really trying to get to know you! I don't even know what you do for a living.

(Beat. Then Tom and Nancy laugh.)

NANCY: Well no wonder you're so therapeutic!

OLIVIA: *(To the empty chair.)* You're a shrink?

NANCY: That's what he just said.

OLIVIA: I might need a referral.

(Lights down.)

SCENE 4. THE THIRD "FIRST BLIND DOUBLE DATE"

OLIVIA: I'm getting really discouraged.

NANCY: I know, but you have to hang in there!

TOM: One of these days you'll have to see one of them. It can't just keep happening.

NANCY: And until that day, we will be here for you! Looking at them for you. Reporting on whether they're appropriate.

OLIVIA: You guys are so wonderful. I don't know how to thank you.

TOM: It's our pleasure.

NANCY: Our entertainment!

TOM: Look on the bright side, Olivia, absence makes the heart grow fonder, yes?

OLIVIA: I think absence just makes the heart . . . feel pathetic.

TOM: They say it makes the heart grow fonder.

NANCY: Tom. Leave her be —

OLIVIA: Yeah, but they also say "Out of sight, out of mind."

TOM: That's true too.

NANCY: *(Staring at the empty chair.)* These things work out Olivia. Look at us.

OLIVIA: I do look at you. You guys met when you were teenagers.

NANCY: We were eighteen.

OLIVIA: Like I said, teenagers.

    (Olivia looks upset. A beat. Adam enters.)

TOM: Are you Adam?

ADAM: Yes.

OLIVIA: You're there! I mean, you're here.

ADAM: You sound surprised. Am I late? I'm sorry I got a little held up at work.

TOM: Hi Adam. I'm Tom. This is my wife Nancy — and *this* is Olivia.

ADAM: Oh wow. This is going to sound strange but . . . You're all so pleasant and attractive! I have to say when Sally said it was a "first blind double date," I was a little anxious about what I might find here.

NANCY: We were anxious too. Some of the people you meet this way . . . they're . . .

OLIVIA: Barely visible.

ADAM: Oh I hate that! When people are invisible.

OLIVIA: I know!

ADAM: But seeing people, hearing them — these things are so subconscious. And I've given up on trying to order around my subconscious. It's too exhausting. My subconscious . . . is like one of those really smart butlers in a British movie? And I'm like the dumb lord of the manor? Why even pretend I'm in charge when it's so obvious who's running the show.
    (Tom and Nancy and Olivia all laugh together.)

OLIVIA: My subconscious is more like a drill sergeant!

NANCY: Mine's like a legal secretary!

(They all laugh again.)

TOM: Mine is like a bicycle messenger!

(More laughter.)

Do you realize, we haven't even ordered drinks yet?

ADAM: Oh that's all right, I can get drunk on air.

OLIVIA: Me too.

ADAM: Not many people can. *(Staring at Olivia.)* So who fixed us up again?

OLIVIA: I don't remember.

ADAM: Neither do I.

TOM: Sally. It was Sally.

OLIVIA: Oh I adore Sally.

ADAM: Me too. Though I've never met her. But I've heard a lot about her. I work with her brother at Whoa — the radio station, W-H-O-A.

OLIVIA: You've never met Sally? How is that possible? She said . . . *(sheepishly.)* she said you were good-looking.

ADAM: Perhaps she saw a photograph? No, I don't photograph well.

OLIVIA: Me neither!

(They stare at each other.)

ADAM: Probably she heard me. People tell me I have a good-looking radio voice.

OLIVIA: Huh. That's hard to imagine.

ADAM: *(A little insulted.)* Why?

OLIVIA: *(Backpedaling.)* I mean, I'd say you do have a good-looking voice . . . but it's hard to tell, when you see someone next to you, whether they have a good-looking voice.

ADAM: *(Realizing.)* You know, that could be my entire problem in life?

OLIVIA: And I definitely see you next to me. This is going to sound forward but, you're the first guy I've found . . . rendered visible in a while.

ADAM: Really! Well you are — incredibly visible, yourself.

(Spotlight on Adam and Olivia gets brighter.)

(Tom and Nancy smile at Adam and Olivia.)

(Then lights fade on Tom and Nancy; they "disappear.")

(Only Adam and Olivia are visible.)

(To the audience, and to each other.)

END OF PLAY

PLAYS FOR
FIVE ACTORS

Early Dismissal

VANESSA DAVID

Originally produced by Nora Theatre Company for The 8th Annual Boston Theatre Marathon at The Sanford Calderwood Pavilion at the Boston Center for the Arts, May 21, 2006. Cast: Mary — Stephanie Clayman, Connie — Faith Justice, Aide — Richard McElvain, June — Alice Duffy, Penelope — Mary Klug. Directed by Richard McElvain. Sponsored by Nora Theatre Company, Mary C. Huntington, artistic director.

CHARACTERS

    MARY: thirties to forties
    CONNIE: thirties to forties
    AIDE: any age, can be male or female
    JUNE: belongs to Mary
    PENELOPE: belongs to Connie

SETTING

    A lobby, the walls are covered in "hand turkeys" and potato stamp Christmas decorations

• • •

At rise: Mary is waiting, with her "hand turkey" in hand. Connie enters.

CONNIE: Oh! I can't believe it's snowing again!

MARY: I know.

CONNIE: And they cancelled the bus so I had to leave work early to come here and pick her up!

MARY: I know.

CONNIE: It's DAY care, not half-day care.

MARY: Preaching to the choir.

CONNIE: Sorry. Hi, I'm Connie Johnson.

MARY: Hi, Mary. Mary Buler.

CONNIE: Like Ferris?

MARY: Like Ferris.

CONNIE: *(Seeing her turkey.)* What's that?

MARY: Oh, my turkey. We can take them home now.

CONNIE: June. What a pretty name.

MARY: Yes it is, isn't it.

CONNIE: Oh, how cute! A turkey made from their handprint. How adorable.

MARY: I remember making these when I was little.

CONNIE: I never made turkeys. I did make those baby feet prints — you know, when the windows are all foggy and you press the side of your fist and then make the toes with your finger.

MARY: Oh yeah, I remember those.

CONNIE: Well, let me see which one is mine. *(She starts to look.)*

MARY: Did you use the centerpiece they made for Thanksgiving?

CONNIE: Absolutely. Almost burned the house down too. We forgot the candles were lit and went next door for dessert . . . we got back in the nick of time. The branches were just about to catch.

MARY: Oh no!

CONNIE: Oh yes! That's OK, nothing happened. Oh, here it is, Penelope. Lovely work Penelope. Isn't it amazing just how creative they can be?

MARY: Oh, yes it is.

CONNIE: This has been such an amazing journey. It's so hard but it's so rewarding! Who'da thunk it?

MARY: I know.

CONNIE: I've got a whole fridge covered with these things. She's made me Valentine's cards and jack-o-lanterns and watercolors and she keeps coming home with plants!

MARY: I know, what's with that?

CONNIE: They must have some sort of deal with a garden center somewhere. She keeps coming home with bulbs.

MARY: You can learn a lot from plants, I suppose.

CONNIE: I guess you're right.

MARY: I'm so glad I did this. In the beginning I wasn't sure. I mean, when I was growing up, I never thought I would. But, when it came time, my husband and I sat down and talked about it, and we were . . . Well, I mean, what are ya gonna do? Life happens, you gotta go with the flow.

CONNIE: But most people have no idea — they don't know. Oprah thinks this is hard? Well let me tell you something Oprah . . .

MARY: Oh, I know. The constant questions. "What are you doing? Where are we going? How does this work? Why can't I do that?"

CONNIE: "How do you know that?" My new answer for everything is that I'm omniscient. But then I have to explain that.

MARY: Oh dear.

CONNIE: Oh, it's too much! I have to switch the breaker, you know, in the fuse box, whenever I want to cook something. She almost burnt the house down once.

MARY: Oh, no! On top of the centerpiece almost burning the place down!

CONNIE: Oh — I threw away all the candles. Matches, lighters. If I ever need to start a fire I'll have to bang two rocks together.

MARY: Oh, but there are good times.

CONNIE: Of course!

MARY: Good times, good crafts.

CONNIE: I wonder what we're getting for Christmas. These trees are nice.

MARY: I think they're made from potato stamps.

CONNIE: I hope they don't plant the potatoes. I don't have room.

MARY: Me either!

CONNIE: A wreath would be nice, or something for the top of the tree.

MARY: Oh, that would be nice.

CONNIE: I remember I made a Santa for the top of the tree in kindergarten. We used some kind of cardboard cone and red paint and cotton balls . . . I don't remember what we used for the head, but he did have one. When it came time to trim the tree I was so excited. My Santa was going to the top of the tree. My mother had a different idea. We always had the angel on top, she said. Santa could sit on the mantle, by the stockings. I remember, pleading with her. He was supposed to go on top of the tree, that's what he was made for. But she didn't listen. He stayed on the mantle. And every year after that, that's where he stayed. I was so happy to throw that thing out when we moved.

MARY: I'm sorry.

CONNIE: Don't be. I suppose it made me a better person, somehow. So this turkey will have its place on the fridge. I'd never do that to her.

MARY: You are a good person.

CONNIE: I tell ya, there's medals for both of us, somewhere.

AIDE: Here they are

(Penelope and June are escorted into the lobby. We see they are not children; they are, in fact, seniors suffering with Alzheimer's.)

JUNE: Where are we?

PENELOPE: Isn't this lovely!

MARY: Hi, Mom.

CONNIE: Hi, Mom. Did you have a good day?

PENELOPE: I don't know. Did I?

AIDE: Yes you did, Penelope. You had a wonderful day.

PENELOPE: Oh, all right then.

JUNE: Where are we going?

MARY: I'm taking you home now Mom. It's snowing, so the bus got cancelled.

JUNE: It's snowing?

MARY: Yup.

PENELOPE: It's snowing? Isn't it lovely.

CONNIE: Yes, yes it is.

PENELOPE: *(Seeing her "hand turkey.")* What's that?

CONNIE: It's a turkey you made out of your handprint.

PENELOPE: How ugly!

AIDE: Penelope, don't say that. It's beautiful.

CONNIE: It's absolutely beautiful. And it's going on the fridge.

PENELOPE: Well, at least I didn't make it.

AIDE: OK Ladies. You have a safe trip home now. *(He exits.)*

PENELOPE: Oh, is that where we're going?

CONNIE: Yes.

PENELOPE: But I don't know how to get there.

CONNIE: That's OK, I do. I'm omniscient.

PENELOPE: Oh, good. Isn't she lovely?

MARY: Yes she is. You've got a wonderful daughter.

JUNE: So do I. I have a daughter.

MARY: Yes you do. As a matter of fact it's me.

JUNE: Oh, well, then it all works out.

CONNIE: It was good talking to you. Have a safe trip home.

MARY: You too.

CONNIE: C'mon Mom. Watch your step.

>   *(Connie and Penelope exit.)*

JUNE: Where are we going?

MARY: I'm taking you home.

JUNE: Where's home?

MARY: Don't worry about it. I've got it all under control. I'm omniscient.

JUNE: Oh, lovely. Oh, look! It's snowing.

MARY: Yes it is, Mom. Yes it is.

>   *(They exit.)*
>   *(Blackout.)*

END OF PLAY

The Cake Women

KEVIN SIX

Originally produced by Da Flye Productions, Kevin Six and Darin Basile, San Diego, Calif., April 2006. Directed by: Kevin Six. Original Cast: Paul — Todd P. Hylton, Diana — Kymri Wilt, Eve — Kellyann Kenshur, Judith — Kristina Meek, Mara — Jessica Moore.

CHARACTERS

    PAUL: self-absorbed, neurotic, clueless

    THE WOMEN (DIANA, EVE, JUDITH, MARA): are not at all alike in appearance or neuroses but similar in their romantic approach

SETTING

    Lighting, music, movement and a bed, up center, suggest all locations

TIME

    The past

. . .

Preshow music: "Tra Le La Le La Triangle," Patsy Cline

SCENE 1. DIANA

Music: "My Baby Thinks She's a Train," Asleep at the Wheel
Paul enters left.

PAUL: . . . because I do. I just do.
    (Diana enters Right.)
DIANA: Well I wish you wouldn't. I don't deserve it.
PAUL: Be that as it may, I can't change the way I feel.
    (The action begins to resemble the circling and head bobbing of pigeons mating.)
DIANA: I can't either. I don't know why . . .
PAUL: Because you know what's good for you.
DIANA: Or what's bad most likely.
PAUL: Me? Little 'ol me? No way. I'm good . . . OK I'm bad. No, I'm so bad I'm good again.
    (Diana hesitates, spoiling the dance.)
PAUL: Are you thinking what I'm thinking?
DIANA: Yes.
PAUL: Do you want to leave?
DIANA: I just know he's right for me.
PAUL: And I'm bad again.
DIANA: He hasn't heard from me in three days. He keeps leaving messages on my machine . . .

PAUL: Unplug it.

(*They resume the dance.*)

DIANA: I've gotta go.

PAUL: I know.

DIANA: I think he's the one. It feels right. I told you how I feel. I've got to give this a try.

(*They are removing each other's clothes and getting into bed.*)

PAUL: The try. And I'm chopped liver again.

DIANA: I need to go and call him. I need to sleep alone.

PAUL: I love you. More than he can. More than there is love.

DIANA: Why?

PAUL: And you love me.

DIANA: I've given up those words.

PAUL: I still love you.

DIANA: But why?

PAUL: I don't know. Because I do. I just do.

(*Lights fade to black.*)

SCENE 2. EVE

Music: "Cry For Me," The Blasters
Paul and Eve are side-by-side in bed as the lights come up.

PAUL: I have something to tell you . . .

EVE: Me too.

PAUL: You have something to tell you?

EVE: No you. I have something to tell you too.

(*They laugh, then . . . *)

PAUL: I love you.

EVE: I'm engaged.

(*Blackout.*)

SCENE 3. EVE'S WEDDING

Music: "My Tears Are Nothing," Brave Combo. Lights and Rumba music up to festive brightness. Eve stands center in a wedding dress with dollar bills pinned to it. Paul enters, pins a bill, they dance. They've done this before.

PAUL: Nice little song.

EVE: I didn't choose it. I didn't.

PAUL: I never thought a stupid song could make you need to puke.

EVE: Paul, you promised. You said you could handle it.

PAUL: I lied, I guess. I guess I lied and I'm not as strong.

(He breaks off but comes back to whisper . . .)

PAUL: This is supposed to be the happiest day of your life, right? This is what you want. I thought it was just in the nightmare that I ruin your wedding. I'm sorry.

(They both make pretend niceties as Paul exits and Eve makes ready for another dancer. The lights fade.)

SCENE 4. JUDITH

Music: "Can't Stand Losing You," The Police. Paul is in the bed with Judith as the lights rise.

PAUL: I'm sorry.

JUDITH: You know, I put up with a lot. I mean in this day and age you know?

PAUL: I'm sorry.

JUDITH: I mean what do you take me for? Did you think I wouldn't find out? Paul, I love you. Don't you understand? I want you. If it's just sex you want, give it to me. I mean just fuck the snot out of me, you know? I mean I just don't understand—

PAUL: No. I don't understand! I don't understand how you could say that—

(Phone rings. Judith answers as Paul shuts up. They've done this before. Light change.)

(As Judith talks on the phone, Paul gets up.)

PAUL: It's strange, really. I don't know why I love these women . . .

(Diana and Eve enter sharing cake.)

PAUL: Why I love these women? Why I love these women.

EVE: Have some Wedding Cake, Paul.

PAUL: No thanks, Eve. Oh, hi Diana. How's — ?

DIANA: Paul, you know. You're like my cream puff. He's my bran muffin, you know?

(Paul gets back into bed as Diana and Eve exit. Lights re-set.)

PAUL: It's all cake to me

(Judith has hung up the phone.)

JUDITH: He'll be home in twenty minutes. You'd better go.

PAUL: I don't understand how you could say that. A married woman.

JUDITH: I want you all to myself.

PAUL: And you want me to remain true to you . . . ?

JUDITH: My cake and eat it too.

PAUL: A married woman with an infant —

JUDITH: Toddler —

PAUL: Child for Christ's-fucking-sake. You know what you want? You want it all. You want your cake and eat it too. I've got a club you can join.

JUDITH: You better go, babe.

PAUL: I know.

JUDITH: I love you.

(Paul gathers his clothes and exits as lights fade.)

PAUL: I love you too.

SCENE 5. MARA

Music: "Train in Vain," The Clash
Paul and Mara are back-to-back in bed, half-asleep.

PAUL: You know what?

MARA: What?

PAUL: I've been in love before.

MARA: Yeah?

PAUL: Yeah.

MARA: Me too.

PAUL: Yeah, I know. Steven.

MARA: Yeah, Steven.

(She is echoed from offstage.)

EVE: Steven.

DIANA: Steven.

JUDITH: Yeah, Steven.

PAUL: Yeah. Well, I want to tell you something . . . I love you.

MARA: Yeah?

PAUL: Yeah. Not like your average, everyday love either. I love you with all my heart, forever . . .

MARA: That's sweet, you know?

PAUL: Yeah?

MARA: Yeah. And when you meet the girl you're gonna' marry, she'll really like hearing that . . . Good night, Steven.

(And Mara is asleep.)

Paul bolts up in bed.

PAUL: No, no, no, no, no, no, no! You're the one . . .
  (Judith enters, followed by Eve, followed by Diana.)
JUDITH: No. I'm the one.
EVE: No. You're married. I'm the one.
DIANA: No you're married. I'm the one.
PAUL: No! *(Indicates Mara.)* She's the one.
  (The Women surround the sleeping Mara on the bed. They become a chorus.)
WOMEN: None of us is the one.
PAUL: Oh Yeah?
WOMEN: Yeah.
MARA: I'm trying to sleep, here.
WOMEN: Have some cake.
  (They again share cake. Mara joins the chorus.)
PAUL: None of you?
WOMEN: None.
PAUL: Everybody loved someone else more.
WOMEN: Each loved her self more.
PAUL: What about the women who aren't here? In this play?
WOMEN: The same.
PAUL: Carrie?
WOMEN: The same.
PAUL: Emily, Sibyl, Sarah, Bettina, Bianca, Helen, Sophia, Maggie, Mary, Mazie?
WOMEN: The same! Every actress in this town. The same!
PAUL: Ha! What about the non-actresses? Virginia, Camille, Anne, Charlotte, Kandy, Betty, Bonnie, Marsha, Marnie . . .
WOMEN: Ha!
PAUL: Huh?
WOMEN: You didn't love them. You didn't know how.
PAUL: Virginia, Camille, Anne, Charlotte, Kandy, Betty, Bonnie, Marsha, Marnie? But what about Emily, Sibyl, Sarah, Bettina, Bianca, Helen, Sophia, Maggie, Mary, Mazie?
WOMEN: Everyone said they did. No one knew how. At various times, you were all of them.

PAUL: I might have been Mara, Judith, Eve and Diana, but I was never Virginia, Camille, Anne, Charlotte, Kandy, Betty, Bonnie, Marsha, Marnie, Emily, Sibyl, Sarah, Bettina, Bianca, Helen, Sophia, Maggie, Mary, Mazie . . .

WOMEN: Alas, poor victim, glorious and vain! What vanity in victimization too. To have your cake and —

PAUL: Wait a minute! I did NOT want my cake and eat it too. They did! Mara, Judith, Eve, Diana.

ALL: Mara, Judith, Eve, Diana. Mara, Judith, Eve, Diana.

WOMEN: With the Cake Women you suffered. The others suffered because you wanted cake.

(Pause.)

PAUL: *(Sings.)* I've looked at life from both sides now . . .

WOMEN: Have some cake.

(Pause.)

WOMEN: And get a life, would ya?

END OF PLAY

If, When, and Only

MARYANN LESERT

If, When, and Only was presented by the Whole Art Theatre of Kalamazoo, Mich. on September 23 and 24, 2006, as part of an evening of one-acts titled *Burning Love: Ten-Minute Plays Inspired by the Sonnets of William Shakespeare.* The play was produced by Tucker Rafferty and directed by Martie Groat, with the following cast: Mary — Valerie Miller, Counselor — Michael Ray Helms, Henry — Preston Misner, If — Nancy Quasarano, When — Will Elwood.

If, When, and Only was inspired by *Sonnet 49:*

> Against that time, if ever that time come,
> When I shall see thee frown on my defects,
> When as thy love hath cast his utmost sum,
> Called to that audit by advised respects —
> Against that time when thou shalt strangely pass,
> And scarcely greet me with that sun, thine eye,
> When love, converted from the thing it was,
> Shall reasons find of settled gravity —
> Against that time do I ensconce me here
> Within the knowledge of mine own desert,
> And this my hand against myself uprear,
> To guard the lawful reasons on thy part.
> To leave poor me thou hast the strength of laws,
> Since why to love I can allege no cause.
>
> *—William Shakespeare*

CHARACTERS

MARY: married to Henry
COUNSELOR: female or male, the couple's marriage counselor
HENRY: married to Mary
IF: female, guardian of the possibility of ongoing love
WHEN: male, escort to the end of love

SETTING

Present day. A marriage counselor's office. Mary and the Counselor sit in an arrangement of three chairs at left: one chair for the counselor, two chairs for Mary and Henry, though Henry is not occupying his chair. Henry remains right (with If and When) ensconced in his "circle" of thought, watching the interaction between the Counselor and Mary.

PRODUCTION NOTES

For ease of reading, the script is written with female gender references to the Counselor, rather than continuous she/he references. If played by a male actor, all references to the Counselor should be changed from sister/her/she to brother/him/he as appropriate.

•   •   •

COUNSELOR: All right. Did you bring your lists?

(Mary nods. Henry is watching.)

COUNSELOR: Good, well, Mary, let's start with yours.

MARY: Just three.

COUNSELOR: That's right. If you had to, and let's just say for today that you have to, categorize all of your feelings under three big headings.

MARY: The three bags you talked about.

(If and When appear as if they belong. Only Henry notices them, first hearing them, then visually taking notice, eventually addressing them.)

IF: For love's sake, I hate it when they get all tricky like that. Three bags! Really!

COUNSELOR: Exactly. Only three bags, but all with very deep pockets.

WHEN: Straight on, sister! Out with the vague!

HENRY: *(Without looking.)* Shhh!

MARY: It was much more difficult than I thought it would be.

IF: Such a tough concept . . .

MARY: I'd see something, and go to write it down, but then . . .

IF: Love — equals — work.

MARY: I felt so silly.

HENRY: *(Bothered by If and When's noise.)* Please.

COUNSELOR: Did you categorize?

MARY: You've heard them all: the toothpaste in the sink and the different ways we enter checks in a checkbook, or whether or not we've ever dreamed of moving or changing our lives so drastically — just because.

COUNSELOR: Trust your list, Mary.

HENRY: Tell her, Mary. All week, how you've wanted to write things down, but then your eyes and your hand, they wouldn't go along.

MARY: I don't know. It's a feeling, stronger and stronger.

WHEN: Oh, poppycock! List away!

IF: Chant it Mary. Chant it strong! Resist the list, resist the list —

HENRY: Please! I have to hear this. I need to know. I need to hear . . .

IF: That's the spirit! Anything's possible. Anything. And you and me, Henry, we're going to listen for clues. You and me.

(Henry takes full notice of If and When. They take the opportunity to introduce themselves.)

IF: If.

COUNSELOR: State your categories, Mary.

WHEN: When. *(Sarcastic.)* Tell me you didn't see this coming.

HENRY: You know? If and when?

WHEN: It's only a matter of time, buddy. A matter of time.

IF: (*Sad, she gestures to each of them.*) If, when, and . . . (*Toward Mary.*) your only, Henry.

COUNSELOR: Mary.

MARY: Talk. Time. Socks.

HENRY: (*Looking toward Mary.*) There is so much of me, over there.

COUNSELOR: Socks?

IF: (*Sighs.*) And it is so obvious.

MARY: Socks. I know. I know! It sounds so silly.

COUNSELOR: No apologies.

WHEN: Yeah. It sucks to be in the know, hey Mar'?

MARY: I listed talking because of listening, really.

IF: (*To When.*) Why do you have to talk like that?

MARY: So much of talking is really about listening. But that's just it. We don't talk. Not about anything of consequence.

WHEN: (*To If.*) Would you rather I take up whining? How does that go?

MARY: Everything we talk about is safe. Entirely safe.

WHEN: (*Mimicking If.*) Oh, if only!

HENRY: All week she's been looking at me differently.

COUNSELOR: Safe from what, Mary?

IF: You care, Henry. You care, still, so very much, I know you do.

HENRY: (*Irritated.*) Please!

MARY: Anger, I guess. Feelings. I'm not even sure it's that ordained. We just don't talk, or stand close, or pass by each other in the kitchen. Unless it's timed.

HENRY: I wasn't made for you, Mary. I wasn't.

MARY: I know it sounds silly, to notice such a thing, but we only come together at certain times. Breakfast time, dinner time . . .

HENRY: I'm just here.

IF: What about bedtime? Anything to work with there, Henry? (*Pause. To When.*) Are we into pocket number two? She said three, right? Are we on two?

MARY: But the unplanned time, the incidental contact, it's awful —

IF: All right. Talk, time, socks. Are we still on talk?

WHEN: No, no. She's well into time.

HENRY: And now we're talking to a paid professional because we can barely stand to look at each other.

MARY: We barely make eye contact or touch each other in broad daylight. Never accidentally, no.

COUNSELOR: Accidentally. That's an interesting term to apply to communication. What do you think it means, Mary?

WHEN: I'll tell you what it means. She wants. *(Motioning to Henry and himself.)* We're happy in the having. But they, *(Motioning to If.)* they gotta
want.

MARY: I don't know. I get in trouble when I want.

WHEN: Hah! See? Want, want, want.

MARY: All I know is what I don't want.

IF: Exactly! Of course! To fall in love again, Henry!

MARY: What I can't want anymore.

IF: To fall, over and over and over. That's what she wants.

WHEN: *(To If.)* Oh, bag your impish sense of perpetual possibility. Sell it to
someone greener.

MARY: You can want something for so long. Too long.

WHEN: You heard her. Our Henry here is a man of time. He knows what's
coming.

MARY: You can want it so badly that you begin to hate it. It gets ahold of you
and it won't go away, but it won't come back either. It just builds and
builds and builds, until you need it. *(In a wicked whisper.)* And needing
is so different.

HENRY: You, Mary? Needing?

COUNSELOR: Name it, Mary.

WHEN: You've been too comfortable, Henry.

COUNSELOR: Name the need.

HENRY: That's it, isn't it. That's all she can see. Same old Henry.

MARY: This is where it all gets too silly to talk about.

IF: Nonsense! Love is supposed to be silly! Unguided. A'new. Let discomfort
reign!

COUNSELOR: Trust your list, Mary.

MARY: Socks.

IF AND HENRY: Socks?

WHEN: *(Makes a buzzer noise.)* Bullshit detector!

MARY: And I started needing too much.

WHEN: Bullshit detector! *(Makes a siren noise to reiterate.)*

HENRY: *(Quieting When.)* No, wait. Wait! I need to hear this.

MARY: I started taking his shirts out of the clothes basket and putting them
on, missing work so I could sit at home, in front of my computer, in his
shirt. I would lift his shirt to my face and close my arms around myself,
to get that citrus-y man scent around me. *(Pause.)* That's how it happens.

You need so much, and you don't find it anymore, anywhere, together. But in shirts. Shirts, and just shriveling away.

COUNSELOR: Why shirts, Mary.

IF: Has this woman no sense of the obvious?

HENRY: I do the same with her bag. That old, gusseted leather bag. She leaves it all over the house, and I like it. I do. I like it. I'll lay a hand on it, next to me at breakfast, and I know she'll be back. She'll be back and I'll be back and we'll all be back together.

MARY: To take in his presence, I guess. (*Whispering.*) Isn't that odd?

IF: Right down to your scent, Henry, she loves you.

MARY: But it doesn't fade. It's as if that scent, lingering in his shirt, is just the way I feel.

WHEN: Bing-bang-bong! Back to the wanting.

COUNSELOR: Why shirts, Mary? Why socks?

IF: Oh, deliver us from this literal Hell!

MARY: I don't know.

IF: She's trying to hang on, for love's sake! To remember his arms and the trembling and yes! (*Eyeing When.*) The transformative power of love.

COUNSELOR: Try. Take a minute and give yourself that nudge.

WHEN: A boy wants his mother, right? No matter what we say, we want comfort. But a girl, she wants to want. She wants that knight to ride in and in and in.

HENRY: I got comfortable.

WHEN: It's like chemistry, Henry. Love only gets comfortable when it gets converted to something else.

COUNSELOR: (*Coaxing Mary.*) You're safe here.

IF: It doesn't have to be this way!

MARY: There wasn't enough of him, enough of his corny jokes and the way he listened — so intently. There wasn't enough time to be with him.

IF: Do you hear, Henry? She wants you. And that's the beauty of it. You can learn. You can! To keep falling. You can learn to manage love.

MARY: And I would put his shirt on, again, I would, if it weren't a reminder of his socks, and his life, his life walking into my life so much that I can't trust myself anymore. That I could let socks do that to me. It sounds so silly, doesn't it?

COUNSELOR: No.

HENRY: It's not about the socks.

MARY: No?

COUNSELOR: Remarkably — no. It's not that unusual to mention some article of clothing.

MARY: I know it sounds silly, but it's a kind of presence, a presence that doesn't ask me to be a part of his life, it just walks in, everywhere, and then sits there in his socks. Take care of me. Pick me up.

WHEN: *(Close.)* This is when, Henry.

IF: So you lay a sock path to it?

HENRY: *(Firm.)* It's not about the socks.

MARY: But I can't pick them up, don't you see?

COUNSELOR: What do you do with them, Mary?

MARY: Do with them?

COUNSELOR: Have you talked about the socks?

MARY: For years.

COUNSELOR: And Henry says . . .

MARY: He doesn't remember. He doesn't know they're there. He doesn't know how much it feels like he hates me when he leaves them lying on the floor.

IF: For love's sake, Henry! Pick up your socks!

HENRY: This is not about the socks!

COUNSELOR: You have to ask yourself, can someone walk over the same socks you're being asked to side-step day after day, and not notice?

MARY: Why does he hate me?

IF: Let go of your pride, man! Tell her you'll pick up her socks!

MARY: I knew it.

HENRY: Yes.

MARY: But I always saw us reacting, doing something.
(Mary begins to work her way closer and closer to Henry as the two of them come closer and closer to realizing the importance of this moment.)

WHEN: Embrace the certainty, Henry. This is when. *(Pauses for emphasis.)* This is when.

MARY: I always saw us changing into something new, together. Taking one of those dance studio classes, or painting pottery.

WHEN: All that you've known was coming. Whensoever, whatsoever, whichsoever — but always there. This is it, Henry. When.

MARY: He would have, before.

HENRY: *(Quietly, as if in thought.)* I still would, Mary. I still would.

IF: That's right, Henry. Fight. Fight!

MARY: I've toyed with the idea. How we'd end it. How we'd reach that time when we'd ache to be together but couldn't get together.

HENRY: *(To If and When.)* We shouldn't have come.

MARY: I don't want the smell and the taste and the memory of socks.

IF: It's not too late. For love's sake, Henry. Reach out.

HENRY: It's too late, isn't it.

MARY: I don't want it anymore.

WHEN: When isn't it, ay?, by the time we start asking questions.

IF: Don't listen to him, Henry. He's short-sighted. He can't stand something going on and on and on. But you can. You can have something that endures. Reach, Henry!

MARY: But this new ache, it has no direction.

HENRY: *(To When.)* You were right. About falling.

IF: No, Henry! No! He's not the fall guy. I am. I am! See? You can learn to be good at it, managing these ups and downs. Sometimes we need something to be yanked away, so we can fight again. You're testing it out, that's all, letting go. But it doesn't feel so good, does it.

HENRY: No. We knew, all along.

COUNSELOR: Mary?

MARY: I guess I always knew, knowing us, this time would come. That's what I'm really angry about. For not understanding, for not being able to steer myself away, all along. All the nagging and the wet toothbrushes and the nails and screws of all sizes mixed in one tin, and . . . *(She turns, abruptly.)* I don't want to be here anymore.

COUNSELOR: Mary.

HENRY: Mary.

MARY: We shouldn't have come.

IF: Damn you, Henry! Do something. Say something! What you're feeling is a chance!

MARY: We shouldn't have come, Henry.

(At this point, Mary and Henry have come closer than ever to each other, and to understanding the pull of this moment.)

WHEN: *(To Henry.)* It's no use, pal. You're no knight in shining armor. *(To If.)* See, talk about the obvious problem. Once the knight rides in, he's got only one of two choices: ride back out or stay. How's he supposed to keep saving the kingdom if he's stuck at home?

(Henry listens, trying to understand. When clarifies for Henry.)

WHEN: The knight's only a knight when he rides away.

HENRY: *(Looking to When and If and Mary.)* What we want is the ideal, and we can't have it. We can't.

IF: Yes you can. You can! Take this chance, Henry. Take this chance!

WHEN: What are you suggesting? They delude themselves on a daily basis?

IF: We all do! We all do, a little, to get by.

WHEN: We live in a world of outcomes, Henry. No one's fault. Just outcomes.

COUNSELOR: *(Breaking back in, softly.)* Nudge, Mary. Don't back off now.

WHEN: Ups and downs, love a'new. Pff!

IF: Hateful, vile outcome! Reach, Henry! Reach!

MARY: *(As if hearing.)* Henry? What if we had not come?

IF: Damnit Henry. Reach!

HENRY: *(Reaching as Mary turns away.)* Mary.

WHEN: *(To If.)* Yeah, if only you had some magic rewind dust for every time that's happened, huh?

IF: *(Turning on When.)* You're thriving in this culture, aren't you!? People dying to feel some shade of bad! Dropping themselves from planes to hit the mountain on high, jumping from bridges with cords to spring back, just before impact. What's to come back from if not the greatest loss, huh?

HENRY: *(Quieting If as Mary walks away.)* She needs this. *(Gesturing to the Counselor.)* She needs her, to do this.

WHEN: Atta boy, Henry. Take us home.

COUNSELOR: *(As Mary returns.)* Good. Good. I can see you've been working since we talked about nudges.

IF: She thinks she does. *(Moving toward Mary.)* She thinks she does, but it's all too rational, we can—

HENRY: No. *(To If.)* Let her have it.

COUNSELOR: Now, where are you, what are you feeling, right now?

HENRY: *(Pauses. To When.)* I know why you're here.

IF: It matters, Henry. It always matters! What if love is limited? What if there's only so much to go around, and you're throwing it away, wasting it, watching it die, right now? Right this minute!? What if?
(Both the Counselor and Mary turn toward Henry, as if hearing the hanging "What If?")

MARY: What if what, Henry?

HENRY: When and if, Mary. Remember? We owed it to each other to say so. *(Pauses, gathering firmness.)* This is not about lists.

COUNSELOR: Why Henry, yes it is. For Mary it is. At least it is right now.

MARY: No.

COUNSELOR: No?

HENRY: Why we love, remember?

MARY: *(Perplexed.)* Henry?

HENRY: *Why* we love.

MARY: I can't say anymore.

IF: Oh, it's a stomach full of sour!

HENRY: Why we keep loving.

MARY: I started needing too much.

HENRY: *(Goes to Mary and puts his jacket or shirt around her shoulders.)* No.

MARY: And maybe, after years, it's not possible to listen so intently. Our brains skip ahead, even if we're trying.

HENRY: No. *(Pauses.)* If and when and because we want to. That's all there really is.

IF: Oh, Henry.

HENRY: Because we want to.

COUNSELOR: That's quite an insight, Henry. And it would be, even more so, if you were able to organize and present your feelings to Mary as she has. Next week —

IF: Next week!? Preposterous! And you pay for this!?

MARY: You don't have a list *(With an unsaid "do you?").*

HENRY: I don't have a list.

COUNSELOR: Henry, we cannot take the next step without your list.

HENRY: That's what I'm telling you. There is no list.

MARY: Henry.

HENRY: I've spent my entire life with my back turned to this moment, and I can't tell you why either, Mary. Only when. *(Pause.)* I don't have a list. I never have.

MARY: *(They begin to walk off, together.)* Just a shirt.

HENRY: Just a shirt, Mary.

(Henry and Mary exit.)

WHEN: Well! Color me vague, now I'm stumped! Was that an outcome?

IF: If ever that time come. *(Thinking.)* Perhaps. Then again, if she gets a strong enough whiff of that shirt. He did smell awfully nice, didn't he? I know what she means, citrus-y. Mmm.

(If and When begin their exit.)

WHEN: Yeah? Well, even oranges and lemons left lying on the window sill will rot.

IF: That's tomatoes. Tomatoes you put on the sill.

END OF PLAY

The Long Arm: A Farce

ESTEP NAGY

CHARACTERS

MARION: twenty-eight, struggling actor, girlfriend of Hal
HAL: twenty-eight, entertainment lawyer, boyfriend of Marion
BILL: twenty-eight, Los Angeles Police Department officer
TY: twenty-five, Los Angeles Police Department officer
SARGE: LAPD sergeant. Never seen onstage. We hear his voice over the radio Bill carries.

SETTING

Shoulder of a freeway in Los Angeles

TIME

The present

• • •

At Rise: 8 PM. Flashing police lights offstage. Sound: A police siren wails briefly, then dies away. Marion sits in a convertible. Hal squirms behind the wheel.

HAL: *(Bangs the steering wheel.)* Damn it!

MARION: Sometimes you drive really fast without knowing it.

HAL: I was going fifty-eight miles per hour!

MARION: Please try to relax. Maybe a taillight's out.
      (Two LAPD officers enter, one on each side of the car.)

BILL: Evening, Sir.

HAL: What's the problem, Officer? I was at fifty-five on the nose.

BILL: That's correct, Sir — you're a regular test pilot. License and registration.

TY: *(Suppressing a chuckle.)* You too, ma'am.

MARION: *(Reaching for her purse.)* Oh. What do you want mine for?

TY: State of California wants to know who's with Speed Racer here.
      (Ty starts to snicker.)

HAL: *(Handing over his license.)* Officer, I —

BILL: *(To Ty.)* Hal Koskie. Never heard of him.

TY: Hal Koskie. Nah — zilcho. She rings a bell, though. Marion Darrow.

BILL: *(Leans in toward Marion.)* Hey, yeah — I'm having a thing, too! Something with the eyes.

TY: *(To Marion.)* Headshot and résumé, please, ma'am.

MARION: Um, really? OK . . .

(She roots around in the back seat.)

HAL: Officer, if you run my license you'll see that my record is clean —

BILL: Slow down there, Crazy Horse. Hand over your headshot.

HAL: I don't have a headshot.

BILL: *(To Ty.)* Ty, hear that? Doesn't have a headshot.

TY: *(To Hal.)* Know who the last guy to not have a headshot was?

HAL: Who?

TY: *(Barely able to talk from the effort of not cracking up.)* Rodney King!

BILL: *(Busts out laughing.)* That's top five. I swear to God!

    (Talks into his radio.)

    Sarge, you hear that one?

SARGE'S VOICE: *(On the radio.)* Loud and clear. Getcha case of beer for that one.

MARION: *(Handing over an 8x10 glossy.)* Here's mine.

TY: Thank you, ma'am.

    (Re: the photo.)

    Hey, great shot! Soft lighting, sexy but intelligent, just a little naughty. Fabulous.

    (Holds it up.)

    This is what I'm talking about.

BILL: Awwww, yeah. Super.

    (Then to Marion.)

    Who did that for you?

MARION: My cousin. He's a photographer.

BILL: Hey, he's really talented. You got a card or something for him?

MARION: No, but I can write down his number for you . . .

BILL: Great. Thanks.

HAL: Officer, am I going to be charged or cited? Because as I understand the law —

TY: *(Reading the résumé.)* Bill, she's done episodic TV! She was recurring on *Xena: Warrior Princess!*

BILL: *(To Marion.)* No shitsky? Who'd you play?

MARION: Um, Aphrodite, goddess of love?

BILL: YES! OF COURSE!

TY: Right? Right? She did that whole gorgeous-but-unattainable thing. Sort of ne-touchez-moi-pas, you know?

SARGE'S VOICE: *(On the radio.)* But just a little naughty.

TY: So true.

BILL: We love your work.

MARION: *(Genuinely touched.)* Thank you! I mean — I know it's not Chekhov or anything, but I really did try to make it an experience for the audience —

HAL: Officer —

BILL: Such great choices. You were completely relaxed, you had active tasks, you were able to be very private amongst a horde of angry cannibals —

TY: The "Judgment of Paris" episode alone was —

SARGE'S VOICE: *(On the radio.)* Magical.

TY: Oh, yeah. Sarge couldn't believe they canceled you.

MARION: I think it was for the best. Out with the old, in with the new, right?

BILL: I'm hearing that.

MARION: So what are you guys working on?

HAL: *(Interrupting.)* Officer, I'm an attorney and I demand that you tell me —

BILL: *(Pulls out his nightstick.)* Koskie, you have the right to remain silent. Anything you say can and will be used against you in a court of law. If you wish to speak now, you may do so only in demotic French.

TY: That's the French of Racine, tough guy!

HAL: I am a member of the California bar, and I have never —

BILL: *(Into his radio.)* That sound like French to you, Sarge?

SARGE'S VOICE: *(On the radio.)* Pas de tout! Make him walk the line.

BILL: Outta the car, Coriolanus.

HAL: *(Springs out of the car.)* Fine. But can we move this along? We have dinner reservations in fifteen — check, ten — minutes.
(Hal slowly and deliberately walks along an imaginary line to prove his sobriety. Everyone ignores him.)

BILL: Anyway — thanks for asking — what we're working on is this right here. We're moving performance into the realm of law enforcement.

MARION: What a cool idea!

TY: Sure. When the department started to put video cameras on the cars — you know, for safety enhancement —

SARGE'S VOICE: *(On the radio.)* We thought, hey, why not take it Method?

BILL: *(Points to his car, toward the house.)* See, there's the camera. Sarge facilitates on a remote basis, from HQ.

TY: And we're licensed to improv. It's an Actor's-Studio-meets-CHiPs type of thing.

MARION: Fabulous! I was Meisner, myself.

BILL: Yeah, we haven't gone there yet. Sarge is a big Stanislavsky-slash-Strasberg guy, and he gets a little tense about competing schools.

SARGE'S VOICE: *(On the radio.)* You can't be too careful, ma'am. The stage is a harsh mistress.

MARION: Please, call me Marion.

(Done line walking, Hal taps Bill on the shoulder.)

HAL: Officer, if you don't mind, I'd like your name and badge number —

BILL: So do you not speak demotic French, or are you resisting arrest?

HAL: I — But —

TY: That sounds like resisting, Bill.

BILL: That's enough outta you, Koskie! Assume the position!

(Utterly afraid to speak, Hal quickly puts his hands on the car and spreads his legs as if he were about to be frisked.)

TY: Wrong position, Pelican Briefs!

BILL: Assume the Basic Relaxation posture! Do it!

HAL: *(Tries to remember French 101.)* Uh — quoi?

TY: *(Disgusted.)* Doesn't know the posture.

BILL: That's why he's so unconvincing.

TY: Tension is the enemy of truth, Koskie!

BILL: Handle it. I'll cover you.

MARION: Please don't hurt him!

(Ty crosses, takes out his nightstick and pulls Hal off the car. He stands him up and spreads Hal's arms out.)

TY: Now shrug your shoulders — slowly — and roll your head in a circle. OK, not bad. Work your face like you're makin' goo-goo eyes. You feel it starting to loosen up in there?

HAL: Oui.

TY: Say "Aaaaaaaaah." Feel your throat vibrate.

HAL: Aaaaaah —

BILL: He's got that voice thing, Ty. It's all in his diaphragm now.

TY: Koskie, say, "HA!"

HAL: *Pour quoi?*

TY: Because I fucking said so!

HAL: Ha! Ha! Ha!

BILL: Ty, Ty, bring it down, man. Remember: "When lenity and cruelty play for a kingdom, the gentler gamester is the soonest winner."

TY: Right, right! I forgot. Sorry.

MARION: *(To Bill.)* "Thou dost thy office fairly."

BILL: *(Bows.)* "Thanks to your highness."

(Then to Ty.)

Hey, Ty, she knows *Henry V!*

TY: Oh, she's good . . .

MARION: I played Hal in one of those cross-dressing college productions. It meant so much to me, that role — I don't ever get to do stuff like that anymore.

BILL: I love it when the dude looks like a lady.

MARION: You should give it a try sometime.

BILL: Yeah, but getting the guys at the precinct to do even one lousy day of kabuki was like pulling teeth.

MARION: I bet they loved it!

BILL: *(Sotto voce.)* Hey, you think maybe that's why you're with this fucking guy, because his name is Hal?

MARION: Um, I don't know . . .

BILL: But stranger things have happened, right?

MARION: I never thought of that.

BILL: Look, ma'am — Marion — you seem a little tense yourself. Why don't you join him? Work it out a little bit?

MARION: That's a great idea. My neck's all cranky.

(Marion climbs out of the car and begins to do the Basic Relaxation exercise.)

BILL: You, too, Ty. You've had the shpilkis lately, too.

TY: Yeah, thanks, Bill. I could use it.

(Everyone does Basic Relaxation except Bill, who corrects their posture with his nightstick. It's a cacophony of "Ahhhhhh" and "HA" and head rolling.)

BILL: *(Shouts to be heard.)* Come on, people! Active breathing! Let it out!

(Then to Ty.)

Ty, begin your private moment!

(Ty sits down and mimes a personal drama where as a child blocks were stolen from him. Soon he identifies Hal as the culprit.)

BILL: *(Noticing Ty's drama with Hal.)* Ty, extend the exercise if you need to! Be inclusive — don't fight the feeling!

(Ty wordlessly attacks Hal toddler-style, slapping and grabbing.)

HAL: *(Not playing along.)* Arrête! Arrête! Ne touchez-moi pas!

(Meanwhile, Marion's relaxation gets to the point where she begins to weep uncontrollably.)

BILL: Marion, that's excellent! Where does it want to go?

(Ty finally leaves Hal alone and curls up into the fetal position.)

BILL: Arms up, Koskie! HAVE the emotion! Loosen the hips!

(Marion slowly walks up right in front of Hal, who stops his exercise.)

HAL: Don't cry, baby. We'll get you some sea bass.

MARION: I don't love you anymore. This relationship is a farce, and I want a life of tragedy.

HAL: But Marion — sweetheart — that's crazy talk —

MARION: *(To Bill, turning away.)* Would you give me a lift?

BILL: Absolutely.

HAL: Marion, wait —

BILL: Please return to the vehicle, Sir!

(Hal reluctantly gets back in the car.)

MARION: *(Turns dramatically.)* Bonjour, Hal. "Le ciel même a pris soin de me justifier."

TY: *(Re: Marion's speech.)* And the Racine, too. Wow!

BILL: *(Tearing up.)* Marion, thank you so much for that. This probably isn't the right time, but we're getting up a precinct production of *The Seagull* and we would be so honored to have you as a guest artist.

MARION: Bien sûr, mon ami.

(Marion exits.)

(Bill leans on the driver-side door and tears a sheet from his ticket-book.)

BILL: Sir, I'm going to let you go with a warning, but you do have one non-functional taillight on the right-hand side of your vehicle. You should get that looked at ASAP. Drive safely, have a nice day and flights of angels sing thee to thy rest.

SARGE'S VOICE: *(On the radio.)* Let's shag ass, guys. There's a 187 in progress at the Mark Taper.

BILL: *(Into his radio.)* 10-4, Sarge.

(Then to Ty.)

On the double, Ty. We got TV stars on stage again.

TY: They never learn, do they?

(Exit Bill and Ty.)

(Hal remains in the car.)

END OF PLAY

Magician Ben vs. the Wizard Merlin

MICHAEL LEW

Magician Ben vs. the Wizard Merlin was originally produced at
the Ensemble Studio Theatre on March 6, 2007, as part of
the "Ma-Yi/Youngblood Mashup," a joint venture between the
Ma-Yi Writers' Lab and Youngblood (the emerging playwrights'
lab at E.S.T.). The Mashup featured new short plays
commissioned by a company of actors, and this play was commissioned for actor Ben Horner. The production was directed
by the playwright and the cast was as follows: Sarah —
Sarah-Violet Bliss, Ben — Ben Horner, Natalie — Natalie
Kim, Audrey — Audrey Lynn Weston, Merlin — John Hart.

CHARACTERS

SARAH: an amateur magician
BEN: an amateur magician
NATALIE: an amateur magician
AUDREY: an amateur magician
MERLIN: a wizard

SETTING

Amateur Magicians' Day

. . .

Sarah, Ben, Natalie, and Audrey sit together. It's Amateur Magicians' Day.

SARAH: So check this out.

BEN: Go.

SARAH: Think of a card. Are you thinking of one?

BEN: Totally.

SARAH: Are you thinking of one?

NATALIE: Yes, the ten of hearts.

SARAH: You weren't supposed to — it's fine, I knew it — but you weren't supposed to tell me.

NATALIE: Oh, sorry.

BEN: Hey, don't make her feel bad. She didn't know.

NATALIE: Yeah Sarah I didn't know.

AUDREY: I have a card! That um. It's the eight of spades.

SARAH: You guys weren't supposed to tell me!

AUDREY: I didn't know!

NATALIE: Yeah, she didn't know.

SARAH: What do you mean you didn't know I just got finished yelling at Natalie.

AUDREY: Yeah. But I wasn't listening. Because I was trying to think of a card.

NATALIE: *(Defensive.)* I'm sorry — in my defense — I'd just like to say. I didn't know.

BEN: *(Wholly inappropriate yelling.)* Look everybody just calm down!! *(Wholly inappropriate calm.)* This is what this day is for. That's why today is Amateur Magicians' Day. Rookie magic mistakes — like these — are part of the fun of it.

NATALIE: Yeah that means it's OK that I didn't know.

AUDREY: Yeah Sarah! We didn't know and it's Amateur Magician's Day so back off because that's part of the fun of it.

SARAH: OK, just — Ben. You think of a card.

BEN: Six of spades. *(Beat.)* Shit I'm sorry.

SARAH: You guys! You're ruining my trick!

NATALIE: *(Dry.)* He didn't know.

BEN: No wait. Eight. Eight of spades.

AUDREY: That's my card! You're an amazing magician, Ben.

SARAH: Guys!

BEN: This trick is boring, Sarah. You forgot to bring a deck of cards. Who comes to Amateur Magician's Day without a deck of cards?

SARAH: But if you'd just give me a chance to . . .

BEN: Nobody wants to see your stupid no-card card trick, Sarah. It's too played out. But I have a trick. Would you like to see it?

AUDREY AND NATALIE: OK!

SARAH: But what about . . .

BEN: OK. What's red and green and craves attention?

NATALIE: I don't know — what?

SARAH: That's not a magic trick! That's a riddle.

BEN: Oh shit. Yeah I guess that's more of a riddle than a magic trick.

AUDREY: You can tell it to us anyway, if you want to.

SARAH: Doesn't anyone want to see my trick? *(She sits down, dejected.)*

BEN: OK OK what's red and green and craves attention?

MERLIN: *(Sauntering in.)* A Christmas ham.

BEN: HEY! You stole my magic trick.

MERLIN: Magic trick? HA! You call that a magic trick?

SARAH: Well it's really more of a riddle . . .

AUDREY: *(Simultaneously with below.)* Who are you?

MERLIN: *(Simultaneously.)* Don't you know who I am? *(He grimaces.)*

AUDREY: *(Simultaneously with below.)* No I don't know who you . . .

MERLIN: *(Simultaneously.)* I am the . . . *(He grimaces.)* . . .

AUDREY: *(Simultaneously with below.)* Sorry just tell me who you . . .

MERLIN: *(Simultaneously.)* Tremble for I am the . . . *(He grimaces.)* I am the Wizard Moilin!

BEN: Moi . . . Moilin? Marlin.

MERLIN: Mellon?

BEN: Melanin?

MERLIN: Melatonin!

BEN: Merlin?

MERLIN: Merlin! That's it. *(As before.)* I am the Wizard Merlin!

AUDREY: I still don't know who you are.

MERLIN: What do you mean you don't know who I am? I just told you.

AUDREY: Yeah but I was thinking of a card.

MERLIN: I am the Wizard . . .

BEN: Merlin.

MERLIN: MERLIN. Thanks I knew that.

AUDREY: Eight of spades.

NATALIE: Are you here for Amateur Magicians' Day?

MERLIN: Amateur? HA! My wizardly powers harness the plasma of the Sun and the cheese of the moon. My pinky has more capacity for thaumaturgical prestidigitation than the . . . the . . .

BEN: The what?

MERLIN: I dunno I kinda blew the load on "thaumaturgical prestidigitation." Point being I am powerful. Powerful beyond your imagination. So no, I am not here for *Amateur Magician's Day.*

NATALIE: Hey, I didn't know!

MERLIN: I'm here to DESTROY Amateur Magicians' Day!

NATALIE: *(Gets up, incensed.)* Hey don't shut me out. I said I didn't know!

BEN: *(Whispering.)* Wait, what'd he say about destroying Amateur Magicians' Day?

AUDREY: *(Whispering.)* I think that's pretty much what he said.

NATALIE: *(Yelling at Merlin.)* I demand that you apologize for acting like I should know you're not here for Amateur Magicians' Day, even though I didn't know.

MERLIN: Silence!

NATALIE: No *you* silence.

MERLIN: Very well. You've provoked my wrath.

SARAH: *Nice work, Natalie.*

NATALIE: *(Whispering.)* I didn't know! *(She sits.)*

MERLIN: With my macabre powers . . .

AUDREY: What's macabre?

BEN: I think it means like when you sculpt things out of newspaper and paste.

SARAH: That's maché!

BEN: Huh. I guess I don't know what macabre is. Wizard Merlin, what's "macabre"?

MERLIN: Silence! With my macabre powers I will now slow time!

ALL BUT MERLIN: *(Slow.)* Hoooooolyyyyyyy Shiiiiiiiittttttt.

MERLIN: Now I will speed up time.

ALL BUT MERLIN: *(Fast.) HOLY SHIT.*

MERLIN: Now I will fill the air with helium.

ALL BUT MERLIN: *(High.)* HOLY SHIT!

MERLIN: Now I will again slow time. BUT! I will also make everyone talk like Scooby-Doo.

ALL BUT MERLIN: *(Slow and like Scooby.)* ROOOOOLLLLLYYYY RIIIIIII-ITTTT.

MERLIN: HA! Tremble before me, minions. Tremble before my awesome macabre powers.

AUDREY: I still don't know what macabre is.

MERLIN: No seriously, though, you guys should get crackin' with the trembling. *(They tremble.)*

AUDREY: You think you're such a great magician Merlin? I'd like to see you guess my card!

MERLIN: Eight of spades.

AUDREY: Oh my God! He's a witch! Ahhhh! *(She exits.)*

BEN: You . . . you dick!

MERLIN: What?! What did you call the Wizard Merlin?

BEN: This is Amateur Magician's Day. Not slow-down-time day. Why are you being such a dick?

(Merlin turns to the audience. Naturalistic, confessional.)

MERLIN: I was only seventeen. But already I knew I had the magician's bug. The magic fingers. The magic wand-erlust. Street fairs, circuses, birthday parties for seven year olds — you couldn't keep me away from them. The seven year olds. But then I discovered the tricks behind the tricks. The smoke. And the mirrors. The way they stick *two ladies* in the box when they saw the lady in half. The way David Blaine puts himself in a tank full of water and calls it magic. That's not magic — that's a stunt. And also I watched those movies *The Illusionist* and *The Prestige.* Do you remember those movies? Well neither of them did much for me. So I dedicated myself to the black arts. *(Turns to them.)* My magic is real, not like your magician's amusements. If it were up to me, Amateur Magicians' Day wouldn't exist at all.

BEN: Whoa. WHOA! Whoa there, Merlin. You are being a serious dick. How can you just *slam* the art of magic like that? *(He poses.)* Magic takes dexterity and charisma.

NATALIE: That's *Dungeons and Dragons.*

BEN: NO, it's not *Dungeons and Dragons.*

NATALIE: Don't yell at me. I'm just saying. They use dexterity and charisma in *Dungeons and Dragons.*

BEN: Stop misdirecting my monologue.

NATALIE: You stop misdirecting my monologue!

BEN: You don't have a monologue, *Natalie! (Natalie exits, crying. Ben poses as before.)* Magic takes dexterity and charisma. It's not just tricks, it's illusions. It's not just tricking people. It's illusioning people. And it's illusioning yourself into believing yourself about what the world can achieve . . . through illusions.

MERLIN: What are you TALKING ABOUT?!

BEN: I won't have you disparaging the validity or nobility, the veracity or sagacity of Amateur Magicians' Day. I challenge you to a duel.
(Audrey and Natalie reappear Vaudeville-style and gasp. They disappear.)

MERLIN: A duel? You?! You challenge me to a duel?

BEN: Yeah that's right.

SARAH: You're gonna duel him? It's suicide! You've seen him. You know how strong he is! You can't win!

BEN: Thanks for the vote of confidence *Sarah.*

SARAH: *(She dives for cover.)* Don't talk to me — he'll think we're friends and kill me too!

BEN: *(Warming up, shaking his arms.)* All right. I'll draw first. *(He points at Merlin.)* What has buck teeth and won't share his house?

MERLIN: *(Dry, quick.)* A beaver who doesn't give a dam.

BEN: Shit!

MERLIN: OK my turn. Your skin's on fire.

BEN: *(Writhing.)* Oh my god! My skin's on fire! My skin's on fire! It burns. It burns . . . Ahhhh. *(He dies.)*

SARAH: *(She pops up from behind the cover. Respectful, tense.)* Wow. He really shouldn't have fucked with you.

MERLIN: Yep.

SARAH: I mean he was totally outclassed.

MERLIN: Uh-huh.

SARAH: All he could do was tell lame riddles. But you set his skin on fire!

MERLIN: Yeah thanks for the recap John Madden — I was there for the thing.

SARAH: Do you want to see my magic trick?

MERLIN: No.
(It immediately gets awkward.)

SARAH: Oh, OK.

MERLIN: Thanks though.

SARAH: Sure . . .

MERLIN: It's just the uh . . . I don't mean to be rude or anything. No offense.

SARAH: No. None taken.

MERLIN: But the uh . . . yeah I just don't wanna see that . . . right now. So uh . . . All right. You keep practicing.

SARAH: I will.

MERLIN: Great. *(Pointing.)* Oh my God is that Houdini on a Segue?

SARAH: What? *(He does a quick, leaping exit.)* Wow. He disappeared. Ben really shouldn't have challenged that guy to a duel. *(To Ben's corpse.)* Hey Ben: You really shouldn't have challenged that guy to a duel. *(Calling out.)* Hey guys?

AUDREY AND NATALIE: *(Reappearing, Vaudeville-style.)* Yeah?

SARAH: You wanna see my magic trick now?

AUDREY AND NATALIE: No thanks *(They disappear.)*.

SARAH: Oh. OK.

END OF PLAY

Model Home

STEPHANIE HUTCHINSON

Original production: The NoHo Arts Center, 11136 Magnolia Blvd., North Hollywood, Calif. 91601, March 1, 2007. Cast: Elizabeth — Jeannie Danielle Jackson, Boy — Carter Blew, Girl — Jesse Blew, Mom — Brooke Bastinelli, Man\Jim — Adam LeBow. Lisa Soland, Director. *Model Home* had a three-night run by Fire Rose Productions, October 18, 19, and 20, 2007, at Secret Rose Theatre in North Hollywood as a Semi-finalist in ACToberfest. Cast: Elizabeth — Holly Montgomery-Webb, Boy — Cole Fletcher, Girl — Camryn Love, Mom — Erin Neimeyer, Man/Jim — Devin Williamson. Jonathan Levit, director.

CHARACTERS

ELIZABETH: thirties, single, a dreamer
BOY: seven to nine, all-American
GIRL: seven to nine, cute
MOM: late twenties, bubbly actress
MAN/JIM: late thirties/early forties, businessman, began as construction
worker and later founded his own company

SETTING

A model home in Southern California

•   •   •

ACT I, SCENE 1

*Setting: The living room of a fully staged model home in Southern Califor-
nia. At Rise: A weekday afternoon. The present. Elizabeth opens the front
door and enters tentatively. Soft classical music, such as Pachebel's Canon, is
playing.*

ELIZABETH: *(Gasps.)* Ohhh, wow! Look at this! Isn't it gorgeous?
(She looks up.)
The architecture . . .
(She looks around.)
. . . the furnishings!
(She walks over to a brown leather armchair and runs Her fingers over it.)
I guess it's OK to sit . . .
(Beat; She calls.)
Hello? Is anybody home?
(She looks around.)
Since I'm the only one here —
(She sits in the chair.)
Don't mind if I do.
(Beat.)
It looks like Brock Homes thought of everything — fresh flowers,
scented candles, soft music. I love the bookcases and the paintings and
the sofa.
(Beat.)
Of course, 5,200 square feet is a bit too big for just one person . . .

(The music fades; She begins to fantasize; excitedly.)

I know, I could get a pet — maybe a cat named "Socks" or a dog named "Muffin" — or both!

(She stoops down as if calling a pet.)

"Ooh, come here, boy!"

(She goes to the front door and mimics greeting guests.)

I could even have guests over —

(She sings.)

"If they could see me now, that little gang of mine"

(Beat.)

Who actually lives in a place like this? Nobody I know, that's for sure.

(Beat.)

It's so quiet in here,

(Pause.)

but that would change if I had a husband and some kids.

(Wistfully.)

Maybe I'd have a little boy named Timmy or Tommy. He'd be the all-American boy-next-door. I'd do carpool and Little League.

(Beat.)

And, of course, a little girl — I'd call her Kelsey — she'd take ballet lessons and wear a pink tutu —

(At that moment, a boy, wearing a baseball outfit and carrying a bat and ball, enters, along with a girl, dressed in a pink tutu. The boy wears a name tag labeled "Son," and the girl wears one labeled "Daughter." Elizabeth blinks in surprise.)

BOY: Mom! Come on! We'll be late for the game!

GIRL: Hurry up! Ballet starts in fifteen minutes!

(A woman enters from the kitchen, carrying a tray of freshly baked chocolate chip cookies. She is wearing a name tag that reads "Mom.")

MOM: *(To Elizabeth.)* Hi! Would you like some chocolate chip cookies? They're fresh out of the oven.

BOY: I want some!

GIRL: Me, too!

MOM: Now, kids, these are for our guest. *(To Elizabeth.)* Please help yourself.

ELIZABETH: *(Confused.)* Uh, thanks.

(She takes a cookie.)

I'm sorry, I thought I was alone here.

MOM: No problem. I just want to welcome you to our home. My name's Elizabeth. What's yours?

ELIZABETH: *(Shocked.)* Why, that's MY name!

MOM: Well, what a coincidence!

> *(Beat.)*

ELIZABETH: I thought that this was a model home . . . ?

MOM: And . . . ?

ELIZABETH: Sorry, I'm a bit confused.

> *(Beat.)*
>
> I think I'd better leave.
>
> *(She goes to the front door. Mom and Children rush over to prevent Her from leaving.)*

MOM: Oh, please don't. We're just getting acquainted. Kids, did you say "hi" to Elizabeth?

GIRL: *(Shaking Elizabeth's hand.)* Hi. Hope you like our home.

BOY: *(Shaking Elizabeth's hand.)* Yeah, we think it's cool. And today's Mom's birthday!

MOM: You must help me celebrate! I'm just about to cut the cake.

> *(Boy and Girl exit to the kitchen and reenter, carrying a birthday cake with lit candles. They sing "Happy Birthday" to Mom. Elizabeth looks on in amazement. Mom blows out the candles.*
>
> *(To Elizabeth.)*
>
> Don't you just love birthdays and birthday cake? Here, have a slice.
>
> *(She cuts Elizabeth a piece of cake and hands it to Her.)*

ELIZABETH: Mom, I mean Elizabeth, I don't understand. Do you live here?

> *(Mom throws Her head back and laughs.)*

MOM: Oh, you don't know.

ELIZABETH: Know what?

MOM: *(In a serious tone.)* They didn't tell you?

ELIZABETH: Tell me what?

MOM: About the home staging.

ELIZABETH: You mean how it's furnished with all the extra touches?

MOM: Yes. Well, we're part of the "extra touches."

ELIZABETH: What?

MOM: The kids and I are actors, hired to show what life can be like here, to *(Gestures.)* "Put the heartbeat back into the home."

> *(Pause.)*

ELIZABETH: You're kidding.

MOM: No, I'm not.

ELIZABETH: So this is not really an episode of *The Twilight Zone?*

MOM: *(Laughs.)* No.

ELIZABETH: *(Relieved.)* Thanks for explaining. I guess I'm not losing my sanity after all.

MOM: *(Back to bubbly actress persona.)* Now, if you don't mind, I have to go back to the kitchen and cook dinner for the evening crowd. Will you be OK looking around on your own?

ELIZABETH: Sure. I'll entertain myself.

MOM: Thanks for understanding. It was great meeting you. If you have any questions, I'll be in the kitchen. Kids, say "bye" to Elizabeth.

BOY: My room's upstairs. I can show you my new plasma TV.

GIRL: And my room has a ballet barre in it.

(Mom and Children exit to the kitchen. Elizabeth is left alone in the living room.)

ELIZABETH: Wow! THAT was bizarre. Only in L.A.!

(She walks to the window and looks out at the landscaped backyard. A Man enters from the front door, unseen by Her, and stands behind Her.)

Now all that's missing is "Dad."

(Beat. She begins fantasizing again.)

He'd come home after a hard day at work and say —

MAN: *(Calling.)* Honey, I'm home!

ELIZABETH: *(Turns around.)* Oh! You scared me!

MAN: Sorry — I couldn't resist that cue.

ELIZABETH: Cue?

MAN: I was just following your script.

ELIZABETH: MY script? YOU'RE the actor.

MAN: I beg your pardon?

ELIZABETH: Oh, come on. I know that this is all staged. Where's your name tag?

MAN: I don't have one.

ELIZABETH: Did it fall off?

MAN: Like I said, there's no tag.

ELIZABETH: You expect me to believe that?

MAN: It's the truth.

ELIZABETH: Your so-called "wife" is in the kitchen.

MAN: I don't have a wife. I'm single.

ELIZABETH: I met your whole "family." Why don't you just admit it?

MAN: Lady, I don't know what you're smoking, but like I said, I'm single.

ELIZABETH: This really is a clever marketing ploy that you people came up with.

MAN: Huh?

ELIZABETH: I feel so stupid that I was taken in, but, never again!

MAN: Why are you so angry?

ELIZABETH: Why are you pretending not to know?

MAN: Is this an episode of *The Twilight Zone?*

ELIZABETH: That's my line —

MAN: So YOU'RE the actor —

ELIZABETH: NO! I mean that I said the same thing a minute ago. Oh, this is just too weird.

> *(Pause.)*

MAN: Let's change the subject. How do you like the house?

ELIZABETH: Oh, I love it.

MAN: So, are you going to buy it?

ELIZABETH: I couldn't possibly afford a house like this. I'm single —

MAN: Oh?

ELIZABETH: — and this is a family house.

MAN: You've got to dream big.

ELIZABETH: Well, what about you? Are you going to buy it?

MAN: No.

ELIZABETH: Why not?

MAN: I'm asking the questions around here.

ELIZABETH: Says who?

MAN: *(Smiling.)* Says me.

> *(Beat.)*

Look, I'm afraid that we got off on the wrong foot. Let me introduce myself. I'm Jim, and you are?

ELIZABETH: Elizabeth.

> *(They continue shaking hands through the next three lines.)*

JIM: No hard feelings?

> *(Beat.)*

ELIZABETH: No.

> *(Beat.)*

This whole experience has been unusual, to say the least.

> *(Beat.)*

JIM: *(Kindly.)* Well, I don't know about you, but I'm getting hungry.

ELIZABETH: They'll be serving dinner soon.

JIM: Who?

ELIZABETH: OK, I'll just play along with your little game. The "family" which you disavow knowing.

JIM: Actually, I would like to take you out to dinner . . . now.

ELIZABETH: Me?

JIM: What do you say? We can discuss the house some more.

ELIZABETH: That's very kind of you, Jim.

> *(Beat.)*

> I'm sorry that I was rude earlier.

JIM: No worries.

> *(Mom and Children enter; Mom sees only Elizabeth.)*

MOM: Dinner will be ready in about twenty minutes.

> *(She sees Jim.)*

> Oh, hello, Mr. Brock. We didn't expect to see you today.

JIM: And I forgot that today was the test run of your performance. How's it been going?

MOM: So far, so good — ask Elizabeth.

ELIZABETH: *(Slowly, to Jim.)* So your last name is Brock, as in Brock Homes?

JIM: Yeah. I'm the builder.

> *(Beat. To Mom.)*

> Elizabeth and I will be eating out tonight.

MOM: All right then — enjoy your evening!

> *(Mom and Children exit; Jim offers his arm to Elizabeth.)*

ELIZABETH: This really is the most unusual model home!

> *(Jim and Elizabeth exit. Lights fade.)*

END OF PLAY

PLAYS FOR
SIX OR MORE
ACTORS

Rain of Ruin

ELAINE ROMERO

World Premiere Production: Curious Theatre Company as part of *The War Anthology* on March 11 to April 29, 2006. Producing artistic director, Chip Walton; associate artistic Director, Bonnie Metzgar; general manager, Jana Curtis. Cast: Agnes — GerRee Hinshaw, Kenji — Peter Trinh, Japanese Woman — Dee Covington, Her Sister — Karen Slack, Ensemble — Step Pearce, Erik Sandvold* and Tyee Tilghman.* Directed by Bonnie Metzgar.

Denotes a member of Actors' Equity Association.

CHARACTERS

AGNES: Mexican-American, forty-ish

KENJI: Japanese, thirty-six

PRESIDENT HARRY TRUMAN

JAPANESE WOMAN

HER SISTER

ENSEMBLE MEN: Air Force, Robert Oppenheimer

SETTING

Hiroshima, Japan; the Oval office; Nagasaki, Japan

TIME

Present and 1945

•   •   •

Agnes and Kenji make out in the Hiroshima Park alongside the river. It's getting heated. Agnes breaks free, wipes off a kiss. Agnes points at herself for her introduction. She addresses the audience.

AGNES: Agnes. For Agnus Dei. Lamb of God. After the Catholic mass. My Mexican mom can't spell. She thought Agnes was Latin. She gets a little confounded by English, the church, and me.

I am a little blind when it comes to love. Twice divorced. With two degrees in English literature. I once wrote a poem and someone put it in a book. That's a little fact about me. I'm in Japan to teach English. That's English lit-speak for *run away*. Lots of warm attention for the *gai-jin*, the foreigner. But Kenji. Three degrees in English literature. A painter. Large canvasses. Beautiful eyes. Black hair. Kind of counter-cultural. He makes me curious. He makes me look.

(Strung throughout the play, Japanese Woman searches for Her Sister. They wear kimonos.)

JAPANESE WOMAN: Has anyone seen my sister? She seems to be wandering around without her skin.

HER SISTER: Has anyone seen my skin? It was hanging off me like tattered clothes.

AGNES: We met by the river, but every place resonates with history for him. *(Ironically.)* This is supposed to be a picnic.

(Agnes and Kenji together, close. Kenji sounds slightly British. Kenji has a small black photo album.)

AGNES: You're not supposed to be with me. That's what Keiko — Matsui-san says.

KENJI: She's just jealous that you have a Japanese boyfriend and she doesn't have any boyfriend *at all.*

AGNES: You sound British when you say that. I didn't think it would be such a big deal to date another teacher. I know dating a student is —

KENJI: *Dame.* (Bad.)

AGNES: Yes, wrong.

KENJI: I don't fit into Matsui-san's idea of who I should be.

AGNES: *Honto ni?* (Really?)

KENJI: *Honto.*

AGNES: All those years in L.A.?

KENJI: All those years of never getting married.

AGNES: You're not very traditional. Painting on canvasses bigger than your apartment. I mean, who else paints in this country?

KENJI: Painters.

AGNES: But language teachers . . . who dream of painting.

KENJI: Languish . . . in their art.

AGNES: Your English scares me.

KENJI: You don't have an American accent when you speak Japanese. You freak me out.

AGNES: You freak me out that you know how to say, "You freak me out."

KENJI: You have a native ear.

AGNES: Don't flatter me, Ken.

KENJI: Kenji.

AGNES: Does it feel like some act of American imperialism for me to call you Ken?

KENJI: It's not just that.

AGNES: *(Sensing something.)* A former nickname? Given to you by an American girlfriend?

(Kenji takes a beat.)

KENJI: *(Pronounces Teresa in Spanish.) Teresa* from Silverlake. Some women can sleep with a man for six years and then dump him via the Internet. America is a free country.

AGNES: It's a cultural thing.

KENJI: *(Suddenly serious.)* Will you look at them?

(Kenji waits.)

AGNES: Now?

KENJI: If not now, when?

AGNES: I want to look at them, I do. *(To audience.)* But if they're really awful, how will I teach my class? How will I look any Japanese person in the face?

KENJI: *(Beat.)* I can't see you any longer if —

AGNES: Are you threatening me?

KENJI: You can't live in Hiroshima and act like you don't live in Hiroshima.

AGNES: You're very complicated.

KENJI: For a Japanese?

AGNES: You're very complicated. *(Beat.)* The war ended. It was a good thing. I doubt you agree. You have to look at where you're getting your information.

KENJI: I could say the same thing.

AGNES: Siding with Hitler. A country could do better.

KENJI: Two atomic bombs is a lot for any country to swallow. *(Beat.)* My father. I used to scratch his keloid scars. You know the keloid scar, the way the skin raises up —

AGNES: I've seen them.

KENJI: Since you've been here?

AGNES: I just figured that maybe Asian people scarred more easily than other people.

KENJI: *(Gently.)* No.

AGNES: *(Vulnerable.)* Oh.

KENJI: My father's arms would itch. I would scratch them for hours. His arms itched his whole life.

AGNES: *(Getting quiet.)* Yeah.

KENJI: And we figured the liver cancer was from that, too.

AGNES: Yeah.

KENJI: And they were worried about me, and I'm fine, you know.

AGNES: Yeah.

KENJI: And there was the black rain from the radiation.

AGNES: We can talk about Pearl Harbor. The Bataan Death March. Your side committed atrocious unforgivable acts.

KENJI: I just want you to look. I don't think that's asking too much of a lover.

AGNES: Do you want me to feel guilty about something I had nothing to do with? Your ex-girlfriend? The bomb?

KENJI: I just want you to know about the *bombs*.

AGNES: I know your dad got hurt and that makes me feel awful.

KENJI: He was seven.

AGNES: That makes me feel awful. *(To audience.)* I hope for more of a committed relationship than I tell Kenji because it's hard. It's hard to let someone know your hope. Instead, we take opposing views and stare each other in the face, wanting more from each other, but history stands, like a boulder, in between us.

KENJI: If not now, when?

AGNES: *(To audience.)* When I was a kid, we saw the photo of the mushroom cloud. Great blast. War over. End of story. Then you meet a guy you really like and he asks you to gaze with him into the mushroom cloud.

KENJI: I just wanted you to look.

(Kenji exits.)

AGNES: *(To audience.)* I have statistics in my head and I don't know where they came from. I have prejudices in my heart and I don't know where they came from. And when I look at him, I just want to — touch him, because skin, culture, and history aside, Kenji is me. The statistic in my head says the bomb saved a million American soldiers by preventing a ground war in Japan. Their *kamikaze* pilots fought in ways that were subhuman. That's the reason we had to drop the bomb. I question my assumptions.

I read everything I can. I sift through speeches and official records. I must walk barefoot in Japanese soil. I must read their dirt, like tea leaves, to find her truth, Agnes', because she knows a thing or two about living.

(Harry Truman and Robert Oppenheimer enter.)

TRUMAN: "Boys, if you ever pray, pray for me now. I don't know whether you fellows ever had a load of hay fall on you, but when they told me yesterday what had happened . . ."

AGNES: That's President Harry Truman after he learned that President Roosevelt had died.

TRUMAN: "I felt like the moon, the stars, and all the planets had fallen on me . . . I'm not big enough. I'm not big enough for this job."

AGNES: When he inherited the presidency, Truman also inherited the atom bomb. *Atom.* The word once meant that which could never be split, that which was indivisible. Indivisible with liberty and justice for all.

On July 25th, Truman wrote in his diary.

TRUMAN: "We have discovered the most terrible bomb in the history of the world. It may be the fire destruction prophesied in the Euphrates Valley Era, after Noah and his famous Ark."

(Scientist Robert Oppenheimer.)

OPPENHEIMER: When it went off, in the New Mexico dawn, that first atomic bomb, we thought of Alfred Nobel, and his hope, his vain hope, that dynamite would put an end to wars.

TRUMAN: "This weapon is to be used against Japan between now and August 10th. I have told the Secretary of War Stimson, to use it so that military objectives and soldiers and sailors are the target and not women and children."

(Insert: Photos of women and children bomb victims, then, the surrounding hills of Hiroshima.)

AGNES: The Air Force advised regarding the target of Hiroshima.

(The actor who plays Oppenheimer also plays Air Force Officer.)

AIR FORCE OFFICER: "There are adjacent hills which are likely to produce a focusing effect which would considerably increase the blast damage."

AGNES: So, I look to see where they warned the Japanese. I look for the part where we drop leaflets. *(Beat.)* No leaflets. I don't understand why we couldn't have warned them. Supposition Number One. American prisoners of war would have been brought to the intended target for slaughter. We cannot warn the Japanese.

TRUMAN: "Sixteen hours ago, an American airplane dropped one bomb on Hiroshima . . . It is an atomic bomb. It is a harnessing of the basic power of the universe . . . Let there be no mistake; we shall completely destroy Japan's power to make war . . . . If they do not now accept our terms they may expect a *rain of ruin* from the air, the like of which has never been seen on this earth . . ."

AGNES: And then afterward.

TRUMAN: "This is the greatest thing that has ever happened. It's time for us to get home."

(Kenji enters. Kenji tries to hand her the photo album. Agnes pushes it away. Insert: the photo of the high school students receiving oil from the policeman.)

AGNES: Oppenheimer said.

OPPENHEIMER: There is no doubt that we were hideously uncomfortable about being associated with such slaughter.

AGNES: It makes me feel that I have no right to kiss Kenji. It makes me feel I have no right to receive his love. *(Beat.)* Kenji speaks the language of ghosts.

KENJI: "The randomness of what happened has never escaped us. I was standing up here, so I lived. He was standing over there, so he died. He looked too long at the blast, so he is permanently blind. Her kimono had a dark pattern, so she will wear it on her skin . . . forever." Skin hung from their arms as they walked like condemned souls in a Buddhist hell realm. Arms outstretched. Flesh hanging from receded bones.

JAPANESE WOMAN: Has anyone seen my sister? She seems to be wandering around without her skin.

HER SISTER: Has anyone seen my skin? It was hanging off me like tattered clothes. I must have lost it down by the river where I went to find *mizu* — water. Then, I fell in.

(Japanese Woman grabs Her Sister as Her Sister falls into the water. Her Sister's skin peels off like a grape. Kenji hands Agnes the photo of the high school students.)

KENJI: Just one picture.

(Agnes stares at the photo. She breaks down and rapidly looks at more.)

AGNES: *(To audience.)* He takes me beneath the mushroom cloud. He brings me to the ground. Kenji's pictures make it real. *(Beat.)* I imagine the Japanese people on the ground. I hear their polite stutters, the hesitation of their tongues — that they would never want to be too assuming or full of self-pride. We did it to *them*.

(Her Sister addresses Japanese Woman who is disfigured by burns.)

HER SISTER: Sumimasen. Mizu o kudasai. (Excuse me. Water, please.)

JAPANESE WOMAN: *Ano ne.* (Well; *Recognizing Her Sister.*) Hideko-chan? (Little Hideko?) *Doko ni ikimashitaka?* (Where'd you go?)

HER SISTER: *(Realizing.)* Akiko-Chan.

(Her Sister starts to cry.)

JAPANESE WOMAN: *Sugoi ne.* (It's too much.)

(Her Sister looks up, a slight smile amidst pain.)

HER SISTER: *Sugoi.* (It's too much.)

JAPANESE WOMAN: *Gomen nasai.* (I'm truly sorry.)

HER SISTER: *(Apologetic for herself.)* Gomen ne. (Sorry.) Doo shoganai. (It can't be helped.)

AGNES: *Doo shoganai. It can't be helped.* That fatalistic phrase that reflects a culture that accepts the inevitability of its fate whatever it may be.

Before the bombs were dropped, military advisors had anticipated that 20,000 American lives would be lost should the U.S. invade Japan. After the bombs, estimated American lives lost was changed to 1 million, to make us feel better, I suppose.

"A confabulation is an untrue belief or reconstruction that can unconsciously alter events in favor of one's own moral claim."

(Project: "Hiroshima in America: Fifty Years of Denial." Robert Jay Lifton and Greg Mitchell.)

AGNES: I uncover truths that make me tremble. I have unraveled a confabulation.

Nagasaki. Bomb two. Dropped it over the Urakami Cathedral. Nagasaki, the center of Christianity in Asia at the time. The Japanese tell me that the bomb landing there meant they weren't supposed to be Christians. American soldier and filmmaker Daniel McGovern entered the ruins of the cathedral on Christmas Eve 1945. Veiled women with radiation sickness celebrated mass. He recorded them singing. I'm haunted by their voices.

(Project the exterior of the cathedral.)

Even Truman decided against using bomb number three. He didn't want to "kill anymore kids." He underlined parts of this passage in his copy of William Shakespeare's *Hamlet*.

TRUMAN: And let me speak to th' yet unknowing world

How these things came about. So shall you hear

Of carnal, bloody, and unnatural acts,

Of accidental judgments, casual slaughters,

Of deaths put on by cunning and forced cause,

TRUMAN AND KENJI: And, in this upshot, purposes mistook

Fall'n on th' inventors' heads.

AGNES: The Japanese love the Bard!

I take three weeks and absorb everything I can. Then I show up at his apartment. I face my accuser.

KENJI: Thank you . . . for looking.

AGNES: *(Beat.)* Do you think it could work, a Bohemia-fied Japanese man and a whacked-out Mexican-American woman?

KENJI: Probably.

AGNES: *Probably* means 75 percent yes, *maybe* means 50 percent yes, but I've noticed it usually means no. My Japanese teacher filled me in on Japanese adverbs and their numerical equivalents. So, essentially, you are telling me *yes*.

KENJI: Essentially.

AGNES: When you traced your dad's scars, what did you see?

KENJI: Grooves . . . that told a story. Of a man who tried to impart something awful inside his son, so he could change the future. Idealism, burden, historical responsibility, all that.

AGNES: That's quite a load.

KENJI: Will you carry it with me?

(Agnes grabs Kenji's hand.)

AGNES: Is this the hand you paint with?

KENJI: Yes.

AGNES: Will you paint me . . . nude?

KENJI: Maybe.

> *(Agnes stares him down.)*
>
> Probably.
>
> *(That is not a high enough percentage for Agnes.)*
>
> Yes.
>
> *(Agnes smiles and kisses him, and looks out to the audience, regarding Kenji behind her.)*

AGNES: *(To audience.)* There is a day in the future when I'll read something new. A day I will find out that the Japanese Emperor went to Josef Stalin, before the bombs were dropped, and asked him to negotiate peace with the United States. On that day, I'll ask myself, why did we drop two atomic bombs on two cities full of people? Had we spent so much money on the bombs that we felt compelled to try them out? But, luckily, that day has not yet come. So tonight I will make love to my Japanese lover and we will resolve these histories another day.

> *(Run the footage and the haunting sound of the Japanese women singing "Silent Night" in the Urakami Cathedral in Nagasaki as filmed by soldier Daniel McGovern.)*

END OF PLAY

RIGHTS AND PERMISSIONS